746.0465   Knisely, Tom.
KNI
CANCELLED   Huck lace weaving
patterns with color
and weave effects.

HUCK LACE WEAVING PATTERNS

with Color and Weave Effects

TOM KNISELY

STACKPOLE
BOOKS

Guilford, Connecticut

I would like to dedicate this book to my friend Madelyn van der Hoogt. Madelyn opened my eyes and helped me see the beauty of Huck Lace. This old rug weaver was a hard sell, but Madelyn, through her articles and book, *The Complete Book of Drafting*, helped me understand the structure of Huck and why it holds a special place in the history of weaving. Cheers!

Published by Stackpole Books
An imprint of The Rowman & Littlefield Publishing Group, Inc.
4501 Forbes Blvd., Ste. 200
Lanham, MD 20706
www.stackpolebooks.com

Distributed by NATIONAL BOOK NETWORK
800-462-6420

Copyright © 2019 by The Rowman & Littlefield Publishing Group, Inc.

Lace pattern photography by Alan Wycheck
Project photography by Kathleen Eckhaus

All rights reserved. No part of this book may be reproduced in any form or by any electronic or mechanical means, including information storage and retrieval systems, without written permission from the publisher, except by a reviewer who may quote passages in a review.

The contents of this book are for personal use only. Patterns herein may be reproduced in limited quantities for such use. Any large-scale commercial reproduction is prohibited without the written consent of the publisher.

We have made every effort to ensure the accuracy and completeness of these instructions. We cannot, however, be responsible for human error, typographical mistakes, or variations in individual work.

British Library Cataloguing in Publication Information available

Library of Congress Cataloging-in-Publication Data available

Names: Knisely, Tom, author.
Title: Huck lace weaving patterns with color and weave effects / Tom Knisely.
Description: Guilford, Connecticut : Stackpole Books, [2019] |
Identifiers: LCCN 2019011063 (print) | LCCN 2019011462 (ebook) | ISBN
    9780811766876 (electronic) | ISBN 9780811737258 (cloth : alk. paper)
Subjects: LCSH: Lace craft. | Hand weaving. | Lace and lace making.
Classification: LCC TT810 (ebook) | LCC TT810 .K57 2019 (print) | DDC
    746/.04653—dc23
LC record available at https://lccn.loc.gov/2019011063

First Edition

CONTENTS

Introduction

Hello. Thank you so much for picking up my book and letting me tell you about my experience with color and weave effects in my weaving. So often an introduction to a book is dry and straightforward. I want to tell you my story as old friends sitting down with a cup of tea and catching up on our latest weaving projects.

The term *color and weave effects* is a little misleading. Your first thought (it was mine as well) is to think that this is a study of how color and the use of color effects the finished woven fabric. That is, in fact, partially true. My guess is that you have seen fabrics that leave you wondering just how they were woven—for instance, a piece of silk fabric that is sometimes blue and then appears to be orange when you move it just

a little in a different direction. These complementary colors, when woven together (an orange warp and a blue weft), produce an interesting effect in the fabric that is due to weaving these two colors together, but this effect is not what we're talking about here. That is a totally different field of color interaction called iridescence, and one worth studying later in your weaving exploration.

In our study of color and weave effects, I think it is best described as the specific order in which light and dark colored threads are placed in the warp and weft. One of the best examples I know is a pattern called Log Cabin. This is a pattern that many beginning weavers try. It produces dramatic effects on a Plain Weave structure. Wow! You would think that

Log Cabin

after many decades of weaving and hundreds of projects that I would be over it. I fell in love with Log Cabin early on in my weaving journey, and, like your first love, you never forget it. It still makes my head turn when I see an example of Log Cabin.

Now this is really where my color and weave story begins. One day, as I was going through a stack of Japanese fabrics, I came across a piece of Log Cabin patterned fabric. The pattern blocks were tiny in comparison to the examples that I was familiar with. The fabric was woven with fine cotton threads in a natural-colored cotton and indigo-dyed cotton. With the help of a magnifying glass, I was able to see that the pattern blocks were made up of a five-thread repeat: dark, light, dark, light, dark. The pattern blocks all began and ended with a dark thread. This was so different and didn't conform to the normal way of threading Log Cabin as I knew it. I just loved this fabric and had to try weaving an example of my own.

I grabbed a tablet of graph paper and started writing a draft that I thought would work. Since Log Cabin is woven as Plain Weave, I didn't need to thread anything more complicated than a straight draw Twill threading. This is how I always approached threading

Log Cabin. I have designed and woven dozens of pieces in just this manner, but there was something quirky about this rendition. Remember, there are five threads to the pattern block, and each block begins and ends with a dark thread. When I started writing this out on my graph paper using a Twill threading, I found that the pattern repeat was over 20 threads. This made sense to me as a five-thread pattern threaded over four shafts repeats after 20 ends (5 x 4 = 20). Take a moment and look at the illustrated threading draft on page 3. Although this is not all that complicated, I thought there must be an easier way to draft this pattern. I thought about other weave structures that repeat over every five threads, and then it hit me: Huck threads typically over five ends. Huck Lace weaves with regular patterned warp or weft floats on a Plain Weave background. The pattern floats are loom controlled. Now look at the next illustration. This shows a typical way of threading Huck. The first pattern block is threaded 2, 3, 2, 3, 2, and the next is threaded 1, 4, 1, 4, 1. That's the answer to my easy threading draft. By placing the dark threads on shaft 2 and the light-colored threads on shaft 3, the first pattern block begins and ends with a dark

Small Log Cabin

thread. The same thing now happens with the next pattern block. I thread the dark threads on shaft 1 and the light threads on 4, and the second pattern block begins and ends on dark threads. This is repeated across the width of the warp. The tie-up and treadling is for Plain Weave, which is the alternation of odd- and even-numbered shafts, 1 and 3 against 2 and 4. The weft is woven with two shuttles carrying one with a dark-colored thread and the other shuttle a light-colored thread. As I weave the fabric, I must remember the dark, light, dark, light, dark order. So there you have it: a simple threading and treadling for the prettiest little Log Cabin pattern you ever saw.

I have to tell you, I was pretty pleased with myself and warped my loom to weave some dish towels with this new-to-me version of Log Cabin. As I was coming down to the end of the warp, I realized there was enough warp left for a little sampling. Throughout the weaving of these towels, I kept thinking that I had threaded the warp to a Huck threading. A voice in my head, which, by the way, sounds a lot like James Earl Jones, kept saying, "Weave it as Huck." If *you* don't hear voices in your head, don't judge. James and I are a team.

When I was done with that last towel, I re-tied my loom to allow me to weave the last of the warp in three different variations of Huck Lace. One sample wove with warp floats, one sample wove with weft floats, and the last sample had both warp and weft floats alternating. I treadled and wove the samples with the dark, light, dark, light, dark order. The

patterns that resulted were nothing less than marvelous. When I had finished weaving the samples, I removed the fabric from the loom and cut the Huck portion from the Log Cabin part of the fabric. It's been my experience that a Huck fabric comes into its own and becomes more beautiful when it's washed in warm water. So off to the sink I went and washed it in warm soapy water, and before my eyes the fabric took its intended shape and look. Now I wanted to warp my loom again to the same draft and weave more towels, but this time in Huck.

I will never forget that day. What started out as a clever way to thread for Log Cabin ended with a whole new way of looking at and weaving Huck Lace. It had always been my experience to weave Huck in a single color for both the warp and the weft, but from that day on I have thought of and seen Huck Lace with a different set of eyes. It started me off in a new direction of weaving and exploring variations of Huck Lace with color and weave effects. It's my pleasure to share these findings with you, and it's my hope that you will find them as fascinating as I have. Of course, it hardly needs saying that some of the patterns are more impressive than others, but beauty is in the eye of the weaver who looks upon the loom. I hope you turn to these patterns to weave towels, baby blankets, scarves, shawls, or any project that warrants beautiful fabric. Now, my friends, go forth and weave.

Tom Knisely

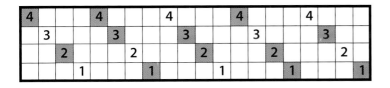

Twill threading

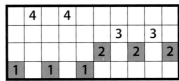

Huck threading

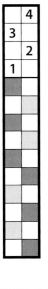

Huck Lace
and How It Weaves

When I think of lace or hear the word *lace*, a particular image comes to my mind. Even after many years of weaving Huck Lace fabrics, when I hear *lace*, it registers as a decoratively patterned fabric that was knitted, crocheted, or constructed as bobbin lace with dozens of individual bobbins interweaving through themselves and creating a cloth that is open or even described as holey.

Huck Lace, however, is a loom-controlled weave structure that, when woven, creates short floats on the surface of the fabric. These fabrics can be described as having warp-way floats on one side of the cloth and weft-way floats on the back. Huck Lace can also weave with both warp-way and weft-way floats on the same surface of the cloth. This makes it unique from other lace weaves, such as Spot Bronson or Bronson Lace, that don't weave this way. Lace weaves are best described as fabric with short floats on the surface of a Plain Weave cloth. The floats are of a repeating pattern and not random. When weaving Plain Weave and the shuttle picks up a thread from the lower layer of warp and forces it to work on the surface, this becomes a warp-way float. If the nose of the shuttle jumps up and catches a warp thread from the upper layer of the shed, that causes a weft float. I remember hearing the story of how Madelyn van der Hoogt consoled a weaver when they discovered that they had made just such an unintentional error. Madelyn passed over it by saying, "Well, look at this way—you have woven an isolated Huck unit." Now I think that is how to make a booboo feel better, don't you?

Now let's take a closer look at this weave structure we have come to know as Huck Lace and see how it works. Huck is a unit weave. This means that there are defined groups of threads that weave as individual units. In Huck, these units are made up of an odd number of threads to the unit. The most common units are five-thread units. You can have as few as a three-thread unit or as many as a seven- or nine-thread unit, but these larger-numbered units are almost never used because the surface floats become too long and catch on things. Of course, this is all relevant to the size of thread you are using for your project. A fine thread sett at 36 ends to the inch could possibly work as a nine-thread unit. The floats would only be a quarter of an inch in length.

On a four-shaft loom, it is possible to have two alternating Huck units. I have seen several different variations of Huck threadings for four shafts, but the one that I like and have used consistently for this book is the one illustrated on page 5. The first unit—I'll call this the A unit—is threaded 2, 3, 2, 3, 2. The second unit—I'll call this the B unit—is threaded 1, 4, 1, 4, 1. A and B units alternately thread across the width of the warp. If a border threading is desired, that weaves as Plain Weave, and a threading of 1, 2, 1, 2, 1 will do the trick. When threading the loom, you must be mindful to alternate the A and B units and to always thread the loom so that the warp also alternates between odd and even shafts so that the fabric weaves as a true Plain Weave. This is also true when threading the border. If the border threading ends on shaft 1, then you will be correct to start the A unit on shaft 2. If the B unit is your last Huck unit threaded, it will have ended on shaft 1. The border threading will have to start with shaft 2. This will maintain the odd and even threading and weave a perfect Plain Weave.

Border   **B Unit**   **A Unit**   **Border**

Now let's look at the illustrated threading draft below. Shafts 1 and 2 make up the Plain Weave border and are also used within the A and B units of the Huck threading. Shafts 3 and 4 make up the pattern shafts. In the A unit, threaded 2, 3, 2, 3, 2, it is the threads on shaft 3 that control the pattern floats. In the B unit, threaded 1, 4, 1, 4, 1, it is the threads on shaft 4 that control the pattern floats. In the weaving of Huck Lace, if these pattern threads are raised during the weaving, a warp-way float is created. If the pattern shaft is allowed to stay down, then a weft float is made.

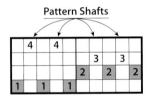

Pattern Shafts

Huck Lace with Warp Floats

Look at the illustration below for Huck with warp floats. In the tie-up you will see the first two treadles are tied in the familiar Plain Weave tie-up. Treadle 1 is tied to lift shafts 1 and 3. The second treadle is tied to lift shafts 2 and 4. Treadle 3 is tied to lift shafts 1, 3, and 4. Treadle 4 is tied to lift shafts 2, 3, and 4. Treadles 3 and 4 are the pattern treadles. Treadle 3 is tied to lift the odd-numbered shafts as well as shaft 4 (4 is a pattern shaft). Treadle 4 is tied to lift the even-numbered shafts as well as shaft 3 (3 is a pattern shaft).

The treadling order of the pattern blocks imitates the threading order. This is known as weaving Tromp as Writ, which simply means to treadle in the same order that the threading draft is written. The first pattern block is treadled 1, 4, 1, 4, 1. Remember, Huck is a Plain Weave cloth with surface floats. The first treadle that you depress, 1, lifts shafts 1 and 3. The second treadle that you depress, 4, lifts shafts 2, 3, and 4. Ah, can you see what is happening? We first wove a pick on the 1 and 3 shed and then followed it with a 2 and 4 shed that also included shaft 3. Shaft 3 is a pattern shaft and is lifted in each of the five pick sequences that make up the first pattern block. This is block A.

The next pattern block, block B, is treadled 2, 3, 2, 3, 2. Treadle 2 lifts shafts 2 and 4. Treadle 3 lifts shafts 1, 3, and 4. In this five-pick sequence, it is shaft 4 that is being lifted in each pick. This makes a warp float in block B.

To weave Plain Weave alone, simply depress the first two treadles alternately. Be mindful, though, to always alternate the odd-numbered shafts with the even-numbered shafts. If your first pattern block starts on treadle 1, treadle 1 lifts shafts 1 and 3. Your last pick of Plain Weave should be on treadle 2,

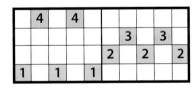

Huck with warp floats

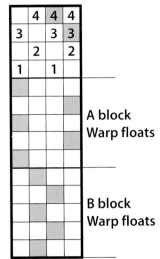

A block
Warp floats

B block
Warp floats

which lifts shafts 2 and 4. If you decide to start your first pattern block on treadle 2, than your last Plain Weave row should be on treadle 1.

Huck Lace with Weft Floats

Now let's look at the illustration for Huck with weft floats. In this tie-up, treadles 1 and 2 stay the same as in the warp float tie-up. These are our Plain Weave treadles. On treadle 3, it is tied to only lift shaft 1. The fourth treadle is tied to lift only shaft 2. To weave an A block, you start the first pick by depressing treadle 2. This lifts shafts 2 and 4. The next pick is on treadle 3. This lifts only shaft 1. With shaft 3 not tied to this treadle, it makes a weft float in the A unit. It weaves with a five-pick sequence. Treadle 2, 3, 2, 3, 2 to weave an A block with weft floats. Then follow

up with the next five-pick sequence of 1, 4, 1, 4, 1. Treadle 1 is tied to lift shafts 1 and 3. Treadle 4 is tied to only lift shaft 2. With the exclusion of shaft 4 from this treadle, it weaves the B block with weft floats. There you have it. Weft floats on the surface of the cloth and the tie-up is lighter to treadle.

Either way you weave it, you will have warp-way floats on one side and weft-way floats on the other side. You can also tie the loom to weave both warp- and weft-way floats on the surface of the cloth, and it allows for some very interesting textures. I have included a number of different tie-ups for your patterning pleasure. My suggestion is to put on a reasonably long warp to sample and try different combinations of both tie-ups and color combinations. Enjoy the weaving.

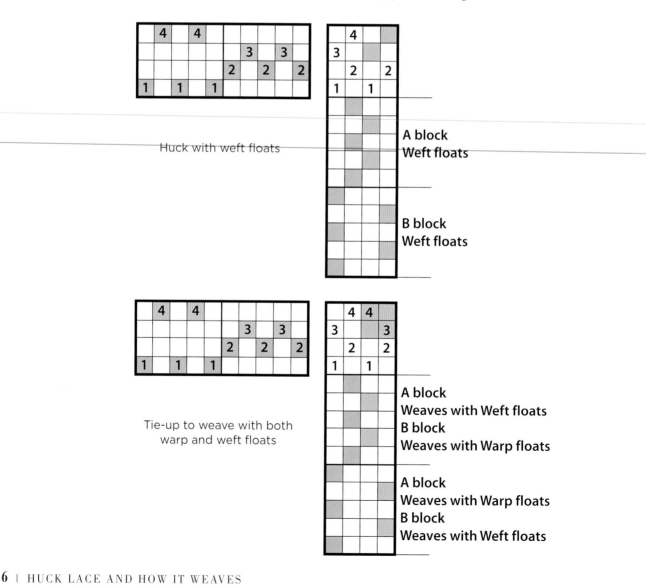

Huck with weft floats

A block
Weft floats

B block
Weft floats

Tie-up to weave with both warp and weft floats

A block
Weaves with Weft floats
B block
Weaves with Warp floats

A block
Weaves with Warp floats
B block
Weaves with Weft floats

Threads and Yarns

Over the years I have looked at a lot of examples of Huck Lace. In my pursuit to collect examples of all forms of antique woven textiles, it is the piles of natural-colored handwoven linens that hold a special place in my heart. I love to spend time on weekends searching through antique shops and going through the linens hoping to find a different example of an early woven textile that I don't already have in my collection. In the case of four-shaft Huck, there aren't many possible variations. Yet holding these ancient pieces of cloth in my hands gives me great pleasure. I wonder who wove them and think about all the hard work in preparing the soil to plant the flax, then harvesting the mature flax straw to ret, break, hackle, and spin into thread so that it could be woven into these plain-looking cloths. Doesn't it make you stand in awe at the thought of how these fabrics came to be? For some people, it's just fabric, but I think these ancient weavers should command a great amount of respect.

When I study the old pieces, there is a commonality: the threads used were fine linen and cotton. Many times the linen threads were single spun and not plied. But cotton threads *were* plied, which makes perfect sense to me. Cotton fibers are short in length and rely on the twist in the spinning and plying to give them strength. In all cases, the threads being used are fine in their size. The very structure of Huck produces warp and weft floats on a Plain Weave or Tabby ground fabric. The floats have a span of five threads in either the warp or the weft direction. Surface floats are subject to catching and snagging. If you are weaving fabric that is intended to be dish towels, you want to avoid those long surface floats. As you dry your flatware, you don't want to have the tines of your forks getting caught under the floats on your towels. In the case of a baby blanket, a surface float spanning, say, three-quarters of an inch might not be all that suitable when little baby fingers and toes can get caught in the floats. So, common sense tells us that we need to keep the surface floats short, maybe no more than a quarter of an inch or less depending on the fabric's intended use. Let's do a little simple math: If a Huck float spans five threads and you want to keep the floats to a quarter of an inch, 5 x 4 = 20, so you will need a sett of 20 EPI (ends per inch). A slightly more open sett (say, 16 EPI) could also work. Taking into consideration that your fabric will shrink a little in the initial washing, a thread that setts at 16 EPI will work just fine.

When choosing a thread for your Huck project, you have a variety to pick from. Like days of old, there are linen and cotton threads of many different sizes and weights. You also have rayon, Tencel, and acrylic yarns at your fingertips. I personally tend to go with natural fibers for towels and table linens, but I might choose rayon or Tencel for scarves or shawls because of the hand and drape that these threads give to the fabric. Wool is a natural fiber as well, and I have on many occasions used it to weave Huck scarves and shawls. The most important thing to remember is that you choose a thread or yarn that is suitable for the project that you want to weave. Whatever the threads or yarns you choose, always be mindful of the length of those floats. As we talked about earlier, the EPI (or ends per inch) needs to be considered. We call this sett. Determining the sett for Huck is easy. Simply take the threads that you have chosen for your project and sett them as if you are going to weave Plain Weave. Remember, Huck is made up of warp floats and weft floats on a Plain Weave background. A closer sett—say, one intended to weave Twill—may not allow you to weave your Huck units to square. If you are feeling unsure about your decision, you should always sample and weave a small piece and wash and dry it to see whether you came to the correct sett.

To find the EPI for Plain Weave, take a ruler and wrap the intended thread around the ruler. Lay the threads so that they touch, side by side, as you wrap for a distance of one inch. Count the wraps, and then divide that number in half. This will give you the correct sett. Forty wraps divided in half is 20 EPI. Now, not everyone will get the same number. Three people all wrapping the same thread might get different answers depending on how loosely or tightly they have wrapped the thread around the ruler. Still, those initial wrappings should be close in number. Let's pretend that you wrapped your thread for the inch on the ruler and the count comes out at 46 wraps. The next step is to divide 46 in half to find the sett for Plain Weave. Your answer is 23. Since 23 EPI is a difficult number to arrange in a reed, go up to 24 EPI and sley two ends in a 12-dent reed. If you think a more open fabric is what you want, sley the reed for 20 EPI, or two ends in a 10-dent reed. Of course, the correct thing to do is sample and weave one at 24 EPI and one at 20 EPI.

Huck is to be woven as a balanced weave. This means that the warp EPI should match the weft PPI, or picks per inch. If you have sett your warp at 20 EPI, then as you weave you are going to do your best to weave so that your beat is going to give you 20 PPI. This is called weaving to square and can be a little challenging sometimes. I would suggest that you warp your loom with an extra yard or so to practice your beat. Try several methods of beating. Try beating with an open shed. Next, try beating with a closed shed, and even try changing the shed before you beat. Practice to see what works best for you to square your fabric. You might want to remove your practice piece from the loom and wash it to see how you did. Washing your sample can make a world of difference. We will discuss more about washing and finishing your fabric in a later chapter. These are some of the best tips I can suggest to you. Sample, sample, and then sample again. You will be glad you did!

How to Read the Drafts

Before you get started, it might be a good idea to understand how to read the drafts for this book. I have written the drafts and tie-ups for the rising shed (or jack) loom. It's been my experience that weavers like this loom for the ease in the tie-ups and treadling. I'm a little old school and have woven Huck on a counterbalance loom, but it was sometimes challenging getting a clean shed. The raising of three shafts to make warp-way pattern floats was not always easy. The same when weaving weft lace and trying to depress three shafts on this sinking-shed loom. I have become spoiled with the ease of weaving on a jack loom. Yet I had to try weaving Huck on a counterbalance loom just to say that I did it and to experience it as did the weavers of years ago. Those old barn frame looms used counterbalance systems. It appears those weavers in the past faced many challenges when weaving Huck, and yet they wove yards and yards of linen fabric in Huck. The existing fabrics prove that point. If you weave on a countermarch loom, you will have no problems. (Counterbalance looms work by suspending the shafts from pulleys, rollers, or horses. Any draft that requires pairs of shafts alternating to create the pattern works well, but when you have a draft that has one shaft working against three, well, the shed is not often clear. This happens with many Huck patterns. A countermarch loom can be tied to cleanly lift one shaft against three or three against one.)

I have written the threading drafts to be read from right to left. I like using numerals to denote the shaft that is to be threaded. Because this is a pattern book of threading drafts that use color and weave effects, you will see that the colors of the squares denote the colors of the threads that are to be placed on those shafts. Pretty straightforward. If there is a curved line drawn below the squares of the threading draft, this is to show the sleying order. When the sett requires that more than one thread is sleyed in a dent, it is useful to show how best to sley the reed. Dark/light, dark/light, dark/dark, dark/light, dark/light. This sequence is then repeated across the warp.

Now let's look at the tie-up. I have written the tie-up to be read from left to right. This means that the first column on the left of your tie-up is to be interpreted

as treadle 1. That column shows the lifting of shafts 1 and 3. When you are using a four-shaft loom, you most likely have six treadles to choose from. The tie-up shows that you are only using four treadles, so you might want to skip the first treadle and assign the second treadle to be treadle 1, and it will be tied to lift shafts 1 and 3. If you are using an eight-shaft loom, you will have 10 treadles at your disposal to choose from. In this case, you might want to skip over several treadles and start your tie-up closer to the middle to make the treadling action easier on your legs and feet. Treadle 2 will lift shafts 2 and 4. Continue tying up your treadles according to the diagram and lift plan. If you have a loom with four shafts and four treadles, you have a loom with what is called a direct tie-up. That means that one shaft is tied to lift with the depression of one treadle. Then, to lift two shafts at one time, you are going have to use both feet at a time. If the pattern requires that you lift three shafts at a time, you are going to have to shift your feet so that two shafts lift with the depressing of one of your feet. Many older looms were built this way, and quite a few weavers like to weave in this manner. The choice is yours.

The treadling order is written so that you follow the lines directly below the tie-up. Read them from top to bottom. Like the threading draft, the treadling order will designate the color of the thread that is to be woven at that time.

Threading   Tie-up

Treadling

The Color
Combinations

The term *color and weave effects*, as we discussed previously, is a little misleading. It conjures up thoughts that you are about to learn the mysteries behind the color wheel and how to successfully put color combinations together. In designing a fabric of your own, a color wheel can be very helpful as a guide. A good color wheel will explain and show the meaning behind words like *monochromatic, complementary colors*, and *triadic color schemes*. Before going out on your own designing, I am going to suggest that you read a good book dealing with the subject of color or, better yet, if you are a visual learner such as I am, please take a class on color theory. It will be well worth your time and may help keep you from making bad color choices and costly mistakes. My daughter Sara seemed to be born with a fabulous sense of color. As a toddler, we would let her dress herself, and Sara had an instinctive knack for putting colors together. It wouldn't be surprising

for her to put on a yellow top, blue shorts, and red cowgirl boots. There, all the primary colors in one fell swoop. It was fun to see her become confident in her choice of outfits. Children seem to do this so easily. As we grow older, we tend to become more conservative because of outside influences. There was a time when you didn't put blue and green together. Red with orange was another. Why? Who comes up with these rules, anyway? If you have ever looked across a green Midwestern cornfield against a blue sky that goes on for as far as the eye can see, well, that is one of the prettiest sights in the world.

For our purposes, *color and weave* is best described as an arrangement of light and dark colored threads that are arranged to a specific order in the warp and also woven in the weft. The most famous and easiest to recognize is the pattern we call Log Cabin. Log Cabin uses two colors in the warp and weft directions. Most two-color combinations will work as long as one color is distinctly dark and the other color light in value. Of course, the combination of black and white will work, but a more interesting pairing might be navy blue with pale yellow. Can you see where I'm going with this?

In the sampling for this book, I wanted to show you what can happen with four different colorways. The first was to thread and weave Huck in a dark color (Black) and a light color (Flaxon) for the warp and weft combinations.

The second combination was a monochromatic theme. This is where you use a dark and light version of the same color. I liked the monochromatic colors of red. Black added to red makes a shade. I chose the color Wine for my dark color. For the light color, I

Flaxon/Black

Wine/Tea

chose a pale pink known as Tea. White added to red makes a tint. Both of these colors of threads share a common base of red.

The third color combination was a complementary color theme. This is where you use a color on the color wheel and look directly across to see the complement. For example, if you choose blue on your color wheel and look directly across from it, you will find the color orange. Doing the same thing, you will find that green is the complement of red, and violet the complement of yellow. A complementary color theme can be tricky sometimes. Complementary colors of the same value or on the same gray scale can produce a muddy look when woven together. For this reason, I picked the colors Garnet and Kelly— Garnet because it was on the darker side of red, and Kelly because it is a lighter and brighter green. I love the way they wove together.

Take a moment and compare patterns of the same draft. Compare the Black/Flaxon patterns on page 16 with the Garnet/Kelly combination on page 112. Even though the patterns share the same structure, there is a different look to the cloth.

Kelly/Garnet

Wine Tone/Pistachio/Tangerine

The fourth color combination I wanted to represent in this pattern book on Huck was a triadic (three-way) color combination. The primary colors of red, yellow, and blue are triadic colors. I wanted to see something a little different, so I chose a dark shade of violet and put it with an orange and a beautiful green. Wow. This was a bit more of a challenge to warp and then weave, but the resulting patterns are so pretty and arguably out of the ordinary.

I found some of the patterns just so-so and some so pretty that I could hardly wait to use the sample as inspiration for the next project. You most likely will do the same. Weave with the attitude that you will have some victories and some disappointments in your color choices. Just stay curious and remember the words of my friend Vonnie, who, when asked by a student whether she liked their color choice, responded with "Why, I'm sure you will find someone who will like it." I love Vonnie's diplomacy.

Finishing Your Huck Fabrics

The washing and finishing of your Huck fabric is going to be much the same as washing and finishing other fabrics. Some warm, soapy water will make all the difference in the final look of Huck. When you are weaving Huck, it is important to do your best to weave the Huck Lace units to square. If the lace units are slightly elongated in height, don't worry. Remember that your warp is under tension and when relaxed the fabric and the Huck units seem to fall right into place. Practice your beat for a few inches to find the beat that best works for you and the materials you are using. Don't be alarmed if you don't see the lace units pop up and stand to attention as you weave. Have faith and carry on. The lace units will appear when you wash the fabric.

I like to hem my towels or twist the fringe on a scarf or shawl before I wash it. This stabilizes the ends, and I don't have to worry that the ends will become undone. For a single item such as a scarf, I will wash it in warm water with a mild soap in the kitchen sink. For a few dish towels, I might throw them into the washer on a regular cycle with a small amount of soap. Then put them in the dryer and treat them as what they are: towels. Do not use fabric softener with towels, because this puts a finish on the towels that makes them soft and not as absorbent. For scarves and shawls, if cellulose-based threads were used, I like adding fabric softener in the rinse. For a wool scarf, try a little hair conditioner in the next-to-final rinse and let it soak for a few minutes; 15–20 minutes is long enough. Finally, rinse again in clear warm water. Then squeeze out the water with your hands or extract the water in the washer on spin only. Hang your scarf or shawl somewhere to air dry. Do not put it in the dryer, as it might felt.

I hope that you enjoy weaving Huck and experimenting with color and weave effects. And I hope that you will love the results of your new journeys as much as I did mine.

HUCK LACE PATTERNS

All samples were woven with
5/2 perle cotton with a sett of 16 EPI.

Huck Lace with Warp Floats

	4		4			
					3		3
				2		2		2
1		1		1		

	4	4	4
3		3	3
	2		2
1		1	

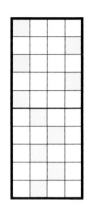

Swatches in this section shown woven with:

Warp: 5/2 cotton

Weft: 5/2 cotton

■ Black

□ Flaxon

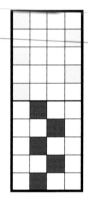

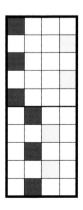

	4		4				
					3		3
				2		2		2
1		1		1			

	4	4	4
3		3	3
	2		2
1		1	

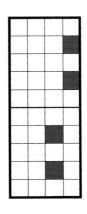

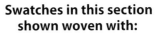

Swatches in this section shown woven with:

Warp: 5/2 cotton

Weft: 5/2 cotton

■ Black

☐ Flaxon

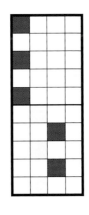

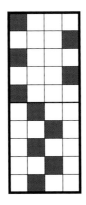

Huck Lace with Weft Floats

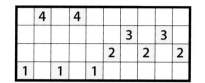

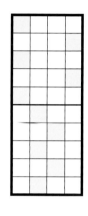

**Swatches in this section
shown woven with:**

Warp: 5/2 cotton

Weft: 5/2 cotton

■ Black

□ Flaxon

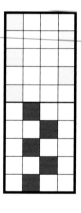

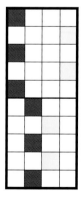

DARK/LIGHT

Huck Lace with Weft Floats

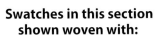

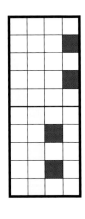

Swatches in this section shown woven with:

Warp: 5/2 cotton

Weft: 5/2 cotton

■ Black

□ Flaxon

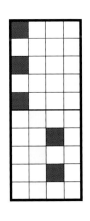

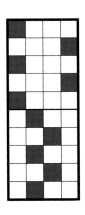

DARK/LIGHT

Huck Lace with Warp and Weft Floats

	4		4				
					3		3
				2		2		2
1		1		1			

	4	4	
3			3
	2		2
1		1	

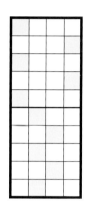

Swatches in this section shown woven with:

Warp: 5/2 cotton

Weft: 5/2 cotton

■ Black
□ Flaxon

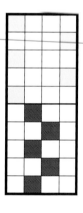

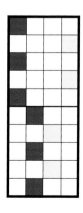

Huck Lace with Warp and Weft Floats

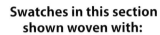

DARK/LIGHT

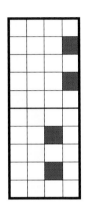

Swatches in this section shown woven with:

Warp: 5/2 cotton

Weft: 5/2 cotton

- ■ Black
- □ Flaxon

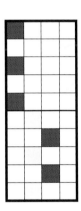

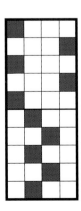

HUCK LACE PATTERNS | **21**

Lacy Huck Squares

	4		4				
					3		3
				2		2		2
1		1		1			

		4	4	
3			3	3
		2		2
1		1		

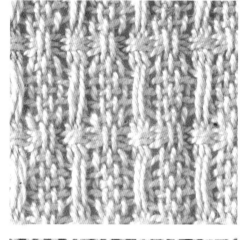

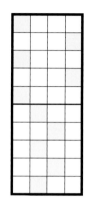

Swatches in this section shown woven with:

Warp: 5/2 cotton

Weft: 5/2 cotton

■ Black

☐ Flaxon

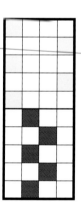

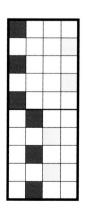

Lacy Huck Squares

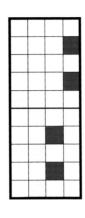

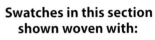

Swatches in this section shown woven with:

Warp: 5/2 cotton

Weft: 5/2 cotton

■ Black

□ Flaxon

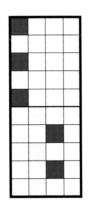

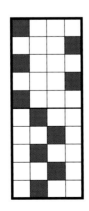

Huck Lace with Warp Floats

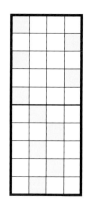

Swatches in this section shown woven with:

Warp: 5/2 cotton

Weft: 5/2 cotton

■ Black

□ Flaxon

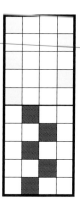

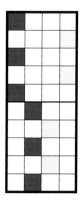

Huck Lace with Warp Floats

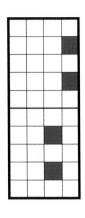

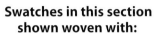

Swatches in this section shown woven with:

Warp: 5/2 cotton

Weft: 5/2 cotton

⬛ Black

⬜ Flaxon

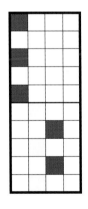

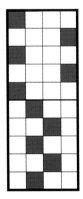

Huck Lace with Weft Floats

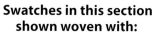

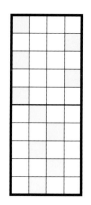

Swatches in this section shown woven with:

Warp: 5/2 cotton

Weft: 5/2 cotton

■ Black

□ Flaxon

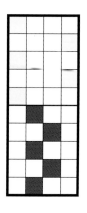

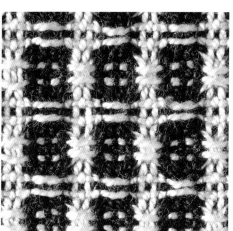

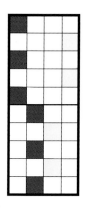

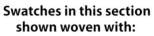

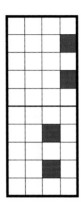

Swatches in this section shown woven with:

Warp: 5/2 cotton

Weft: 5/2 cotton

■ Black

□ Flaxon

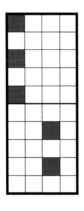

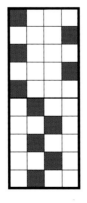

Huck Lace with Warp and Weft Floats

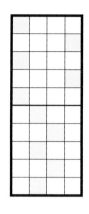

 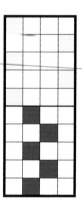

Swatches in this section shown woven with:

Warp: 5/2 cotton

Weft: 5/2 cotton

■ Black

□ Flaxon

 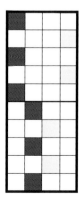

Huck Lace with Warp and Weft Floats

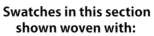

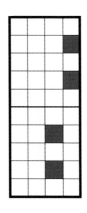

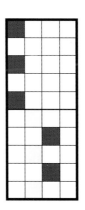

Swatches in this section shown woven with:

Warp: 5/2 cotton

Weft: 5/2 cotton

■ Black

□ Flaxon

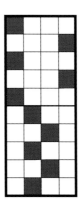

Lacy Huck Squares

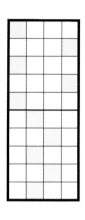

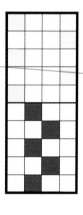

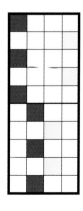

Swatches in this section shown woven with:

Warp: 5/2 cotton

Weft: 5/2 cotton

■ Black

□ Flaxon

Lacy Huck Squares

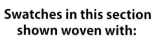

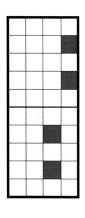

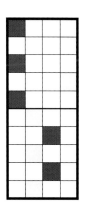

Swatches in this section shown woven with:

Warp: 5/2 cotton

Weft: 5/2 cotton

- Black
- Flaxon

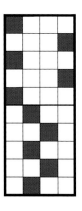

Huck Lace with Warp Floats

DARK/LIGHT

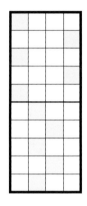

Swatches in this section shown woven with:

Warp: 5/2 cotton

Weft: 5/2 cotton

■ Black

□ Flaxon

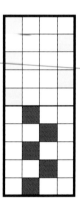

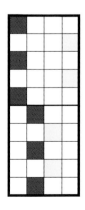

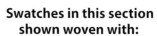

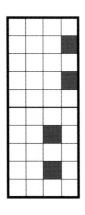

Swatches in this section shown woven with:

Warp: 5/2 cotton

Weft: 5/2 cotton

▇ Black

☐ Flaxon

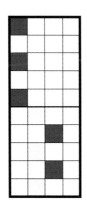

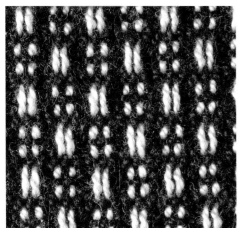

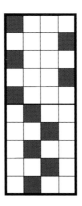

Huck Lace with Weft Floats

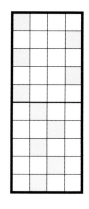
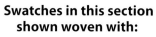

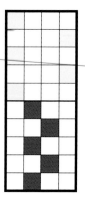

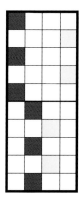

Swatches in this section shown woven with:

Warp: 5/2 cotton

Weft: 5/2 cotton

- ◼ Black
- ◻ Flaxon

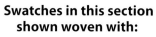

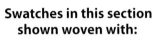

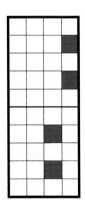

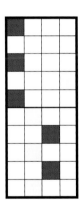

Swatches in this section shown woven with:

Warp: 5/2 cotton

Weft: 5/2 cotton

- Black
- Flaxon

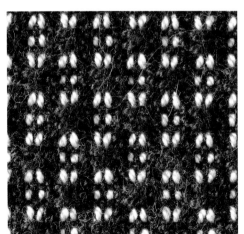

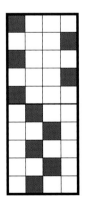

Huck Lace with Warp and Weft Floats

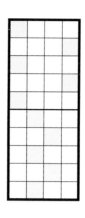

Swatches in this section shown woven with:

Warp: 5/2 cotton

Weft: 5/2 cotton

- Black
- Flaxon

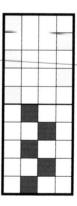

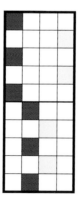

Huck Lace with Warp and Weft Floats

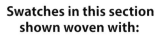

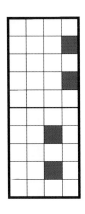

Swatches in this section
shown woven with:

Warp: 5/2 cotton

Weft: 5/2 cotton

▇ Black

☐ Flaxon

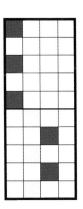

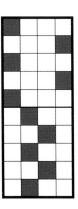

Lacy Huck Squares

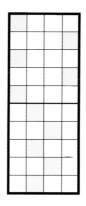

Swatches in this section shown woven with:

Warp: 5/2 cotton

Weft: 5/2 cotton

◼ Black

☐ Flaxon

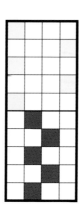

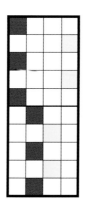

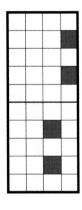

Swatches in this section shown woven with:

Warp: 5/2 cotton

Weft: 5/2 cotton

■ Black

□ Flaxon

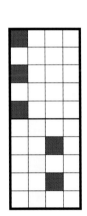

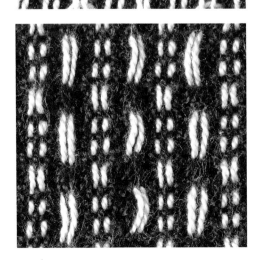
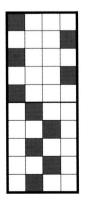

Huck Lace with Warp Floats

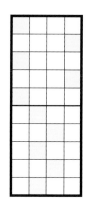

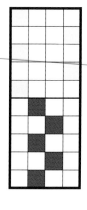

> **Swatches in this section shown woven with:**
>
> **Warp:** 5/2 cotton
>
> **Weft:** 5/2 cotton
>
> ◼ Black
>
> ☐ Flaxon

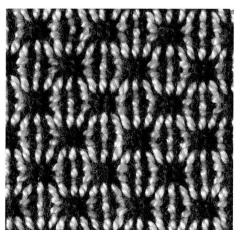

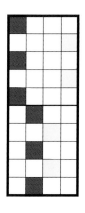

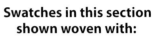

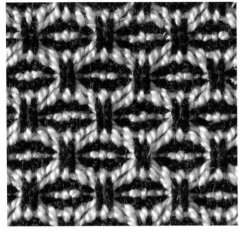

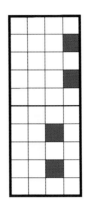

Swatches in this section shown woven with:

Warp: 5/2 cotton

Weft: 5/2 cotton

■ Black

□ Flaxon

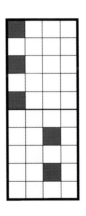

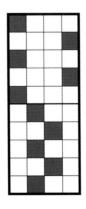

Huck Lace with Weft Floats

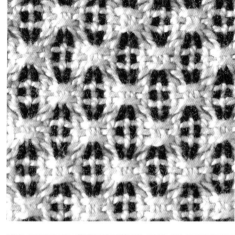

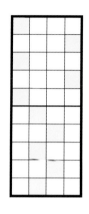

Swatches in this section shown woven with:

Warp: 5/2 cotton

Weft: 5/2 cotton

█ Black

☐ Flaxon

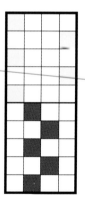

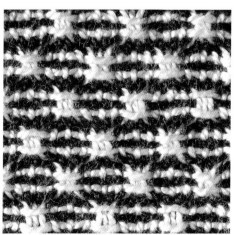

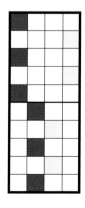

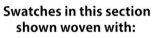

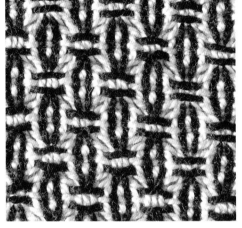

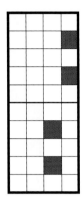

Swatches in this section
shown woven with:

Warp: 5/2 cotton

Weft: 5/2 cotton

■ Black

□ Flaxon

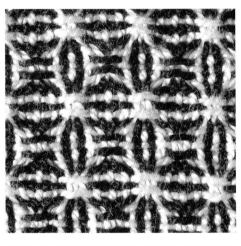

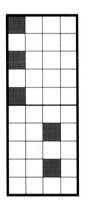

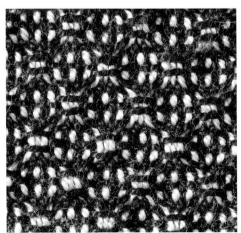

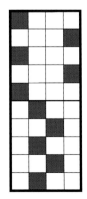

Huck Lace with Warp and Weft Floats

DARK/LIGHT

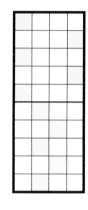

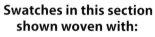

Swatches in this section shown woven with:

Warp: 5/2 cotton

Weft: 5/2 cotton

■ Black

☐ Flaxon

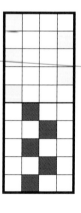

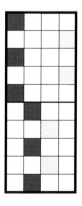

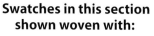

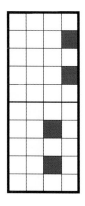

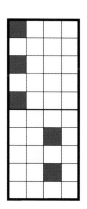

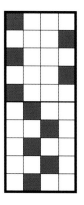

Swatches in this section shown woven with:

Warp: 5/2 cotton

Weft: 5/2 cotton

■ Black

□ Flaxon

Lacy Huck Squares

	4		4				
					3		3
				2		2		2
1		1		1			

	4	4
3		3	3
	2		2
1		1

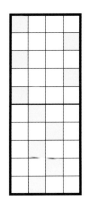

Swatches in this section shown woven with:

Warp: 5/2 cotton

Weft: 5/2 cotton

■ Black

□ Flaxon

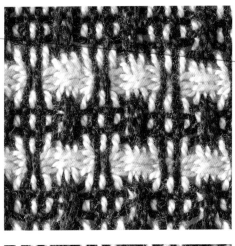

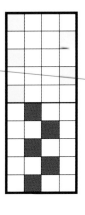

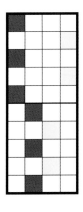

	4		4					
					3		3	
				2		2		2
1		1		1				

	4	4
3		3	3
	2		2
1		1

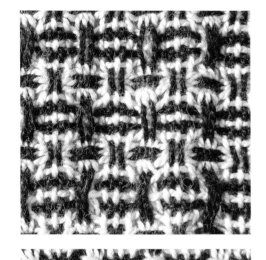
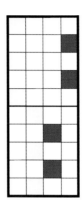

Swatches in this section shown woven with:

Warp: 5/2 cotton

Weft: 5/2 cotton

■ Black

□ Flaxon

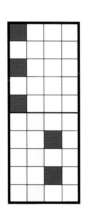

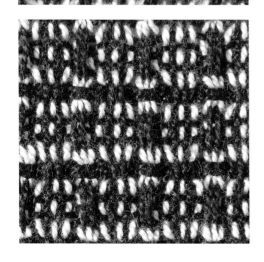
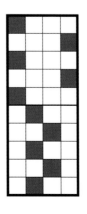

Huck Lace with Warp Floats

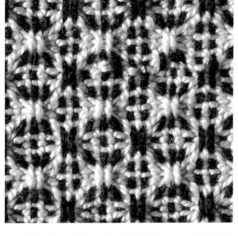

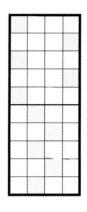

Swatches in this section shown woven with:

Warp: 5/2 cotton

Weft: 5/2 cotton

- ■ Black
- □ Flaxon

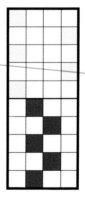

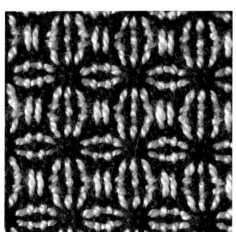

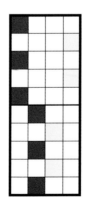

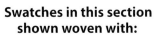

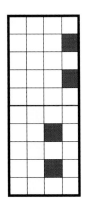

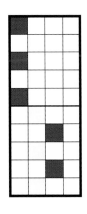

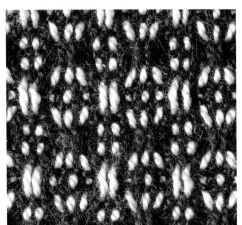

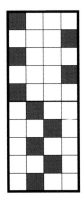

Swatches in this section shown woven with:

Warp: 5/2 cotton

Weft: 5/2 cotton

⬛ Black

⬜ Flaxon

Huck Lace with Weft Floats

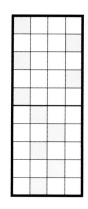

Swatches in this section shown woven with:

Warp: 5/2 cotton

Weft: 5/2 cotton

■ Black

☐ Flaxon

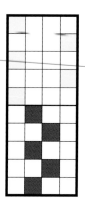

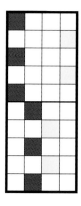

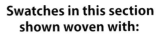

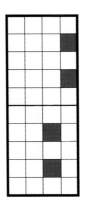

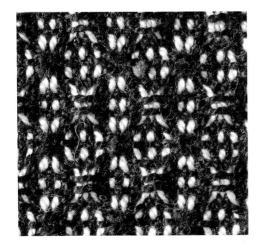

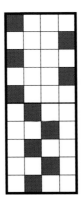

Swatches in this section shown woven with:

Warp: 5/2 cotton

Weft: 5/2 cotton

- Black
- Flaxon

Huck Lace with Warp and Weft Floats

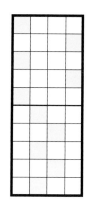

Swatches in this section shown woven with:

Warp: 5/2 cotton

Weft: 5/2 cotton

■ Black

□ Flaxon

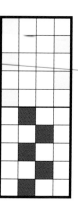

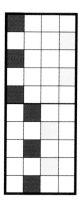

Huck Lace with Warp and Weft Floats

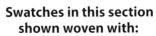

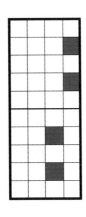

Swatches in this section shown woven with:

Warp: 5/2 cotton

Weft: 5/2 cotton

■ Black

□ Flaxon

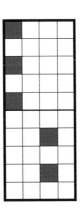

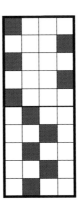

Lacy Huck Squares

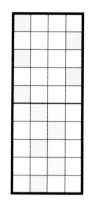

Swatches in this section shown woven with:

Warp: 5/2 cotton

Weft: 5/2 cotton

■ Black

□ Flaxon

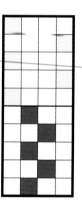

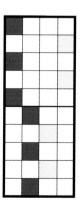

Lacy Huck Squares

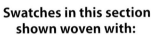

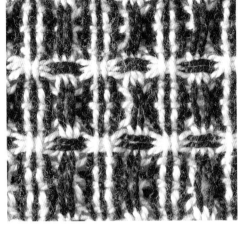

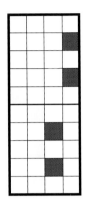

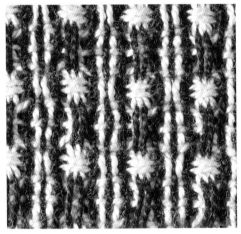

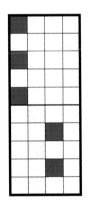

Swatches in this section shown woven with:

Warp: 5/2 cotton

Weft: 5/2 cotton

- Black
- Flaxon

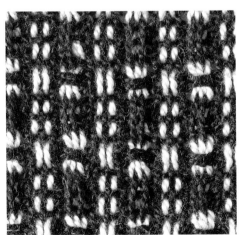

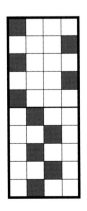

Huck Lace with Warp Floats

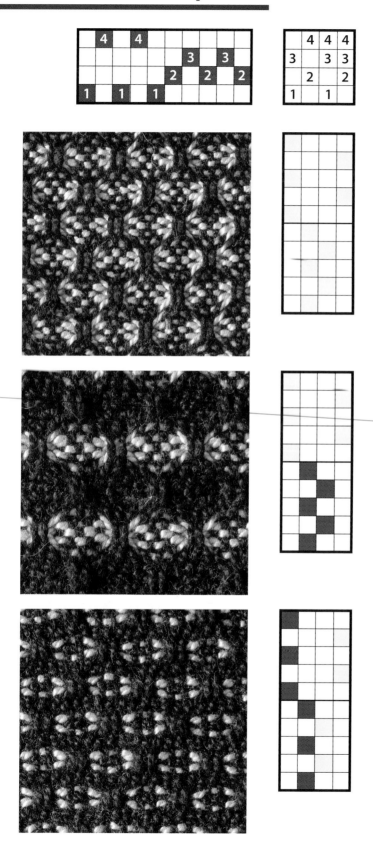

Swatches in this section shown woven with:

Warp: 5/2 cotton

Weft: 5/2 cotton

■ Black

□ Flaxon

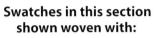

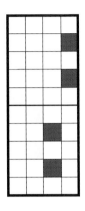

Swatches in this section
shown woven with:

Warp: 5/2 cotton

Weft: 5/2 cotton

■ Black

□ Flaxon

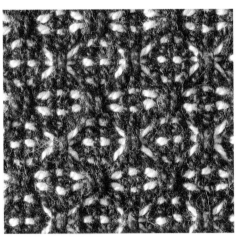

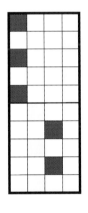

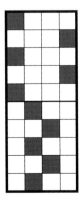

Huck Lace with Weft Floats

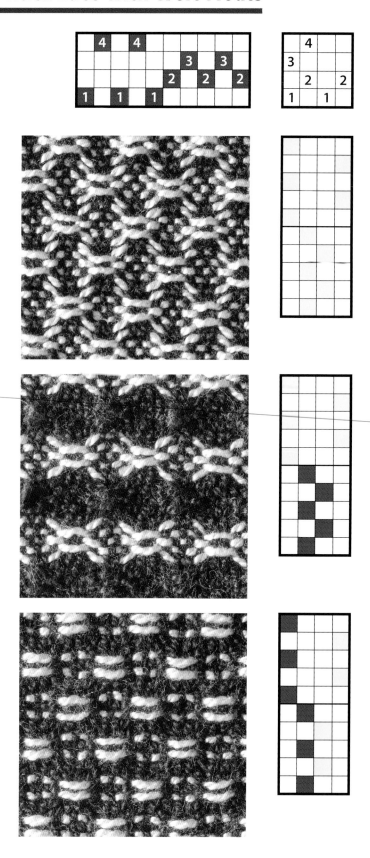

Swatches in this section shown woven with:

Warp: 5/2 cotton

Weft: 5/2 cotton

■ Black

☐ Flaxon

Huck Lace with Weft Floats

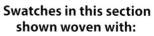

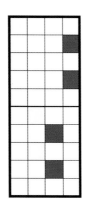

Swatches in this section shown woven with:

Warp: 5/2 cotton

Weft: 5/2 cotton

■ Black

□ Flaxon

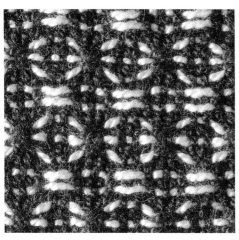

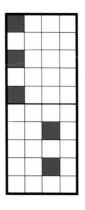

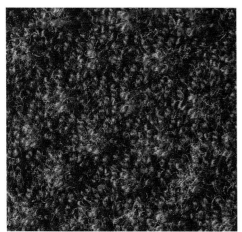

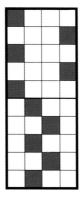

Huck Lace with Warp and Weft Floats

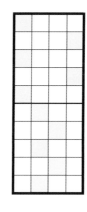

Swatches in this section shown woven with:

Warp: 5/2 cotton

Weft: 5/2 cotton

■ Black

□ Flaxon

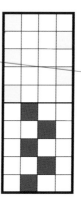

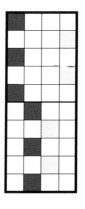

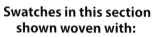

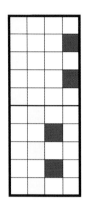

Swatches in this section shown woven with:

Warp: 5/2 cotton

Weft: 5/2 cotton

■ Black

□ Flaxon

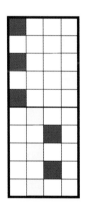

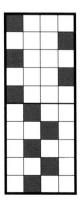

Lacy Huck Squares

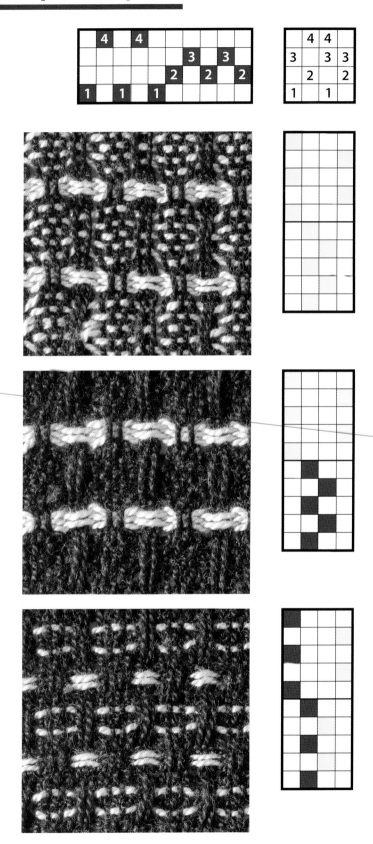

Swatches in this section shown woven with:

Warp: 5/2 cotton

Weft: 5/2 cotton

■ Black

□ Flaxon

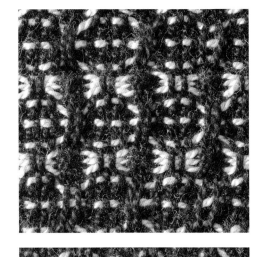

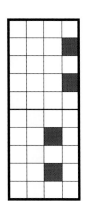

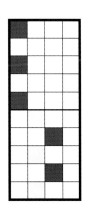

Swatches in this section
shown woven with:

Warp: 5/2 cotton

Weft: 5/2 cotton

■ Black

□ Flaxon

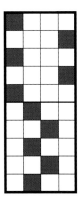

Huck Lace with Warp Floats

MONOCHROMATIC

	4		4				
					3		3
				2		2		2
1		1		1			

	4	4	4
3		3	3
	2		2
1		1	

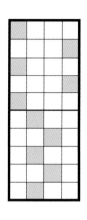

Swatches in this section shown woven with:

Warp: 5/2 cotton

Weft: 5/2 cotton

■ Wine

▨ Tea

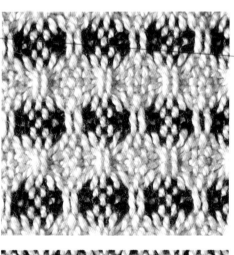

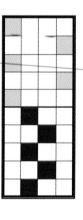

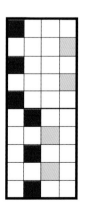

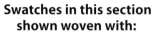

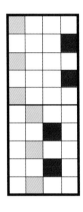

Swatches in this section shown woven with:

Warp: 5/2 cotton

Weft: 5/2 cotton

◼ Wine

◻ Tea

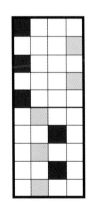

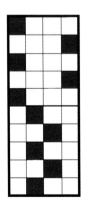

Huck Lace with Weft Floats

Swatches in this section
shown woven with:

Warp: 5/2 cotton

Weft: 5/2 cotton

■ Wine

▨ Tea

	4		4				
					3		3	
				2		2		2
1		1		1				

	4		
3			
	2		2
1		1	

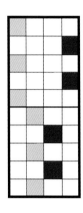

> **Swatches in this section shown woven with:**
>
> **Warp:** 5/2 cotton
>
> **Weft:** 5/2 cotton
>
> ■ Wine
>
> ▨ Tea

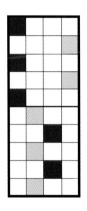

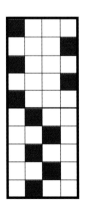

Huck Lace with Warp and Weft Floats

MONOCHROMATIC

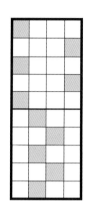

Swatches in this section shown woven with:

Warp: 5/2 cotton

Weft: 5/2 cotton

■ Wine

▨ Tea

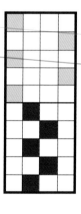

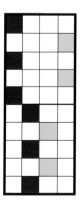

Huck Lace with Warp and Weft Floats

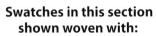

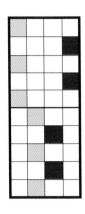

Swatches in this section shown woven with:

Warp: 5/2 cotton

Weft: 5/2 cotton

- ■ Wine
- ▨ Tea

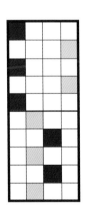

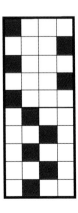

Lacy Huck Squares

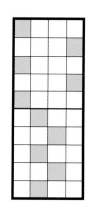

Swatches in this section shown woven with:

Warp: 5/2 cotton

Weft: 5/2 cotton

Wine

Tea

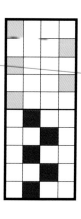

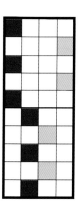

	4		4				
					3		3
				2		2		2
1		1		1			

	4	4	
3			3
	2		2
1		1	

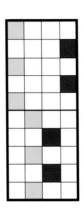

Swatches in this section shown woven with:

Warp: 5/2 cotton

Weft: 5/2 cotton

■ Wine

▨ Tea

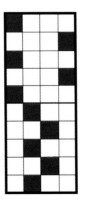

Huck Lace with Warp Floats

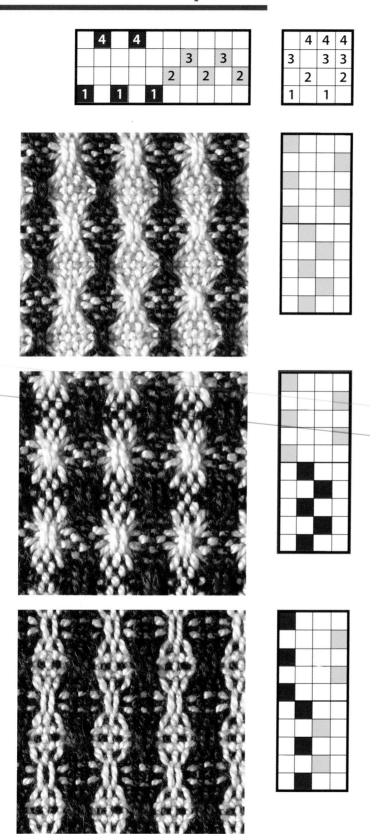

Swatches in this section shown woven with:

Warp: 5/2 cotton

Weft: 5/2 cotton

■ Wine

▨ Tea

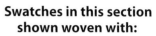

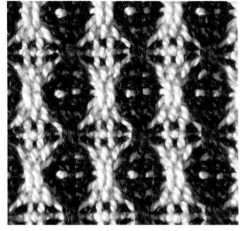

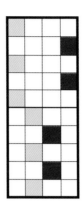

Swatches in this section shown woven with:

Warp: 5/2 cotton

Weft: 5/2 cotton

- ■ Wine
- ▨ Tea

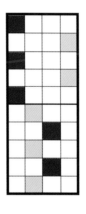

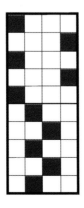

Huck Lace with Weft Floats

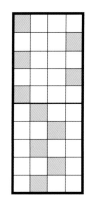

Swatches in this section shown woven with:

Warp: 5/2 cotton

Weft: 5/2 cotton

 Wine

Tea

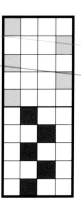

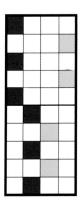

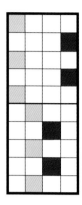

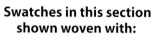

Swatches in this section shown woven with:

Warp: 5/2 cotton

Weft: 5/2 cotton

■ Wine

▨ Tea

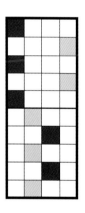

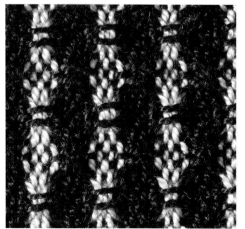

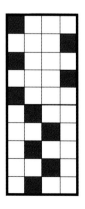

Huck Lace with Warp and Weft Floats

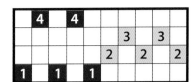

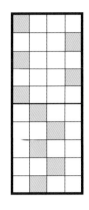

Swatches in this section shown woven with:

Warp: 5/2 cotton

Weft: 5/2 cotton

■ Wine

▨ Tea

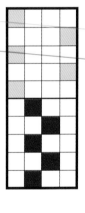

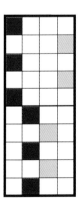

Huck Lace with Warp and Weft Floats

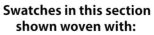

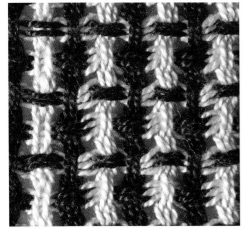

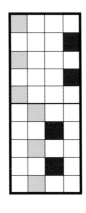

Swatches in this section shown woven with:

Warp: 5/2 cotton

Weft: 5/2 cotton

■ Wine

▨ Tea

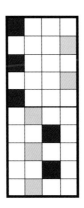

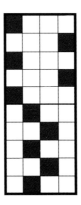

Lacy Huck Squares

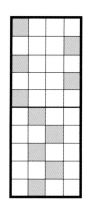

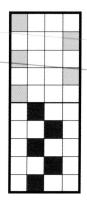

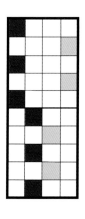

Swatches in this section shown woven with:

Warp: 5/2 cotton

Weft: 5/2 cotton

- ■ Wine
- ▨ Tea

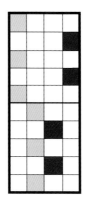

Swatches in this section shown woven with:

Warp: 5/2 cotton

Weft: 5/2 cotton

■ Wine

▨ Tea

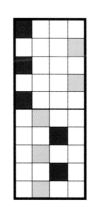

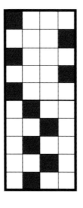

Huck Lace with Warp Floats

MONOCHROMATIC

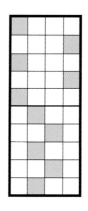

Swatches in this section shown woven with:

Warp: 5/2 cotton

Weft: 5/2 cotton

- ■ Wine
- ▨ Tea

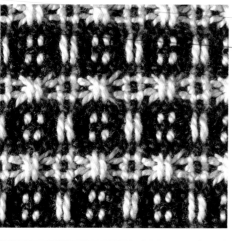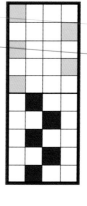

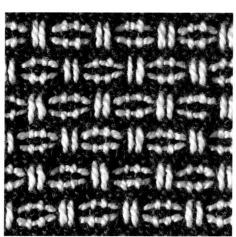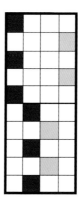

Huck Lace with Warp Floats

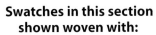

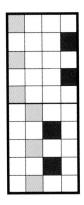

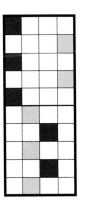

Swatches in this section shown woven with:

Warp: 5/2 cotton

Weft: 5/2 cotton

■ Wine

▨ Tea

Huck Lace with Weft Floats

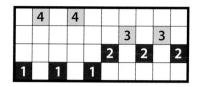

 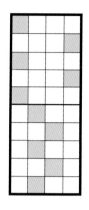

Swatches in this section shown woven with:

Warp: 5/2 cotton

Weft: 5/2 cotton

◼ Wine

▨ Tea

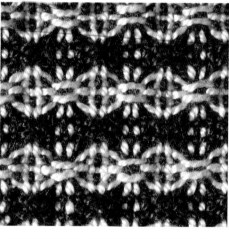 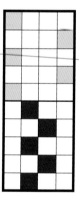

 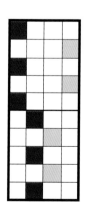

MONOCHROMATIC

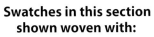

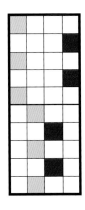

Swatches in this section shown woven with:

Warp: 5/2 cotton

Weft: 5/2 cotton

■ Wine

▨ Tea

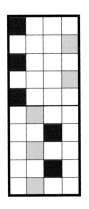

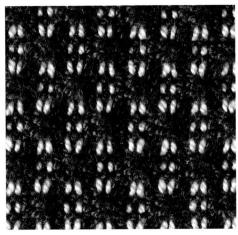

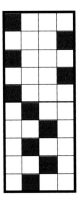

Huck Lace with Warp and Weft Floats

MONOCHROMATIC

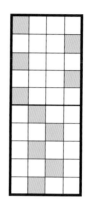

Swatches in this section shown woven with:

Warp: 5/2 cotton

Weft: 5/2 cotton

- Wine
- Tea

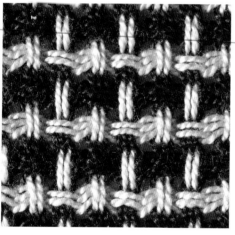

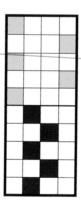

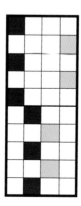

Huck Lace with Warp and Weft Floats

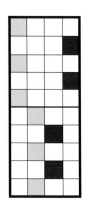

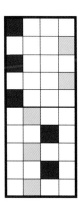

Swatches in this section shown woven with:

Warp: 5/2 cotton

Weft: 5/2 cotton

- ■ Wine
- ▨ Tea

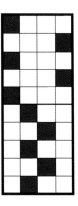

Lacy Huck Squares

MONOCHROMATIC

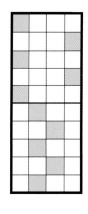

Swatches in this section shown woven with:

Warp: 5/2 cotton

Weft: 5/2 cotton

■ Wine

▨ Tea

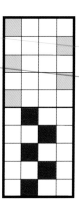

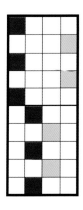

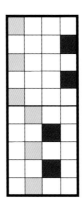

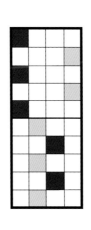

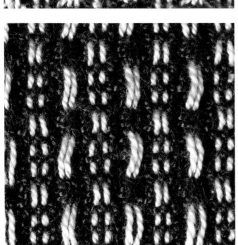

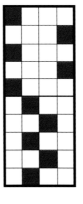

Swatches in this section shown woven with:

Warp: 5/2 cotton

Weft: 5/2 cotton

■ Wine

▨ Tea

Huck Lace with Warp Floats

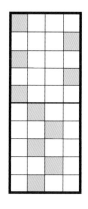

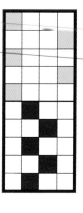

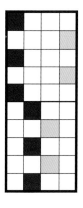

Swatches in this section shown woven with:

Warp: 5/2 cotton

Weft: 5/2 cotton

■ Wine

▨ Tea

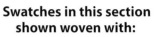

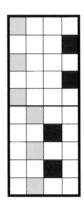

Swatches in this section shown woven with:

Warp: 5/2 cotton

Weft: 5/2 cotton

■ Wine

▨ Tea

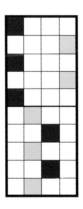

Huck Lace with Weft Floats

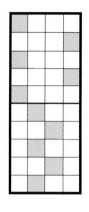

Swatches in this section shown woven with:

Warp: 5/2 cotton

Weft: 5/2 cotton

■ Wine

▨ Tea

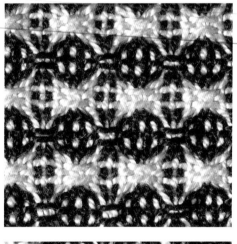

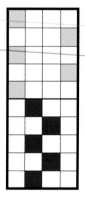

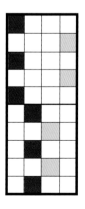

Huck Lace with Weft Floats

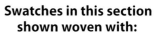

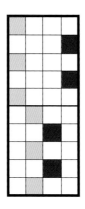

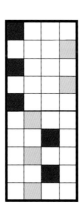

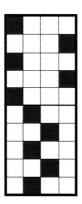

Swatches in this section shown woven with:

Warp: 5/2 cotton

Weft: 5/2 cotton

■ Wine

▨ Tea

Huck Lace with Warp and Weft Floats

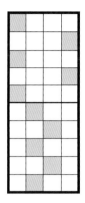

Swatches in this section
shown woven with:

Warp: 5/2 cotton

Weft: 5/2 cotton

■ Wine

▫ Tea

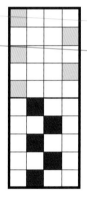

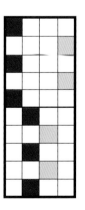

Huck Lace with Warp and Weft Floats

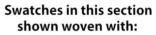

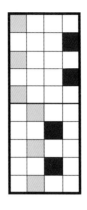

Swatches in this section shown woven with:

Warp: 5/2 cotton

Weft: 5/2 cotton

■ Wine

▨ Tea

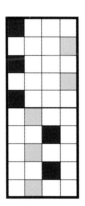

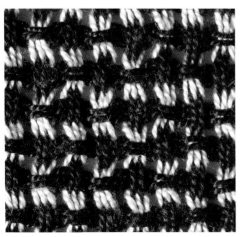

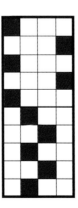

Lacy Huck Squares

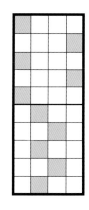

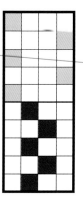

Swatches in this section shown woven with:

Warp: 5/2 cotton

Weft: 5/2 cotton

■ Wine

▧ Tea

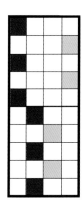

	4		4				
					3		3
				2		2	2
1		1		1			

	4	4	
3			3
	2		2
1		1	

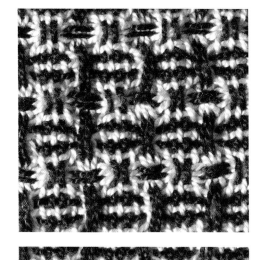

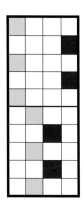

Swatches in this section shown woven with:

Warp: 5/2 cotton

Weft: 5/2 cotton

■ Wine

▨ Tea

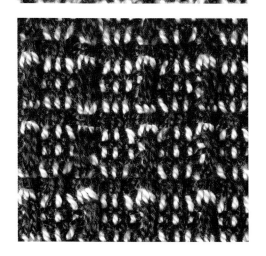

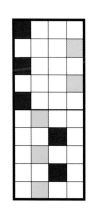

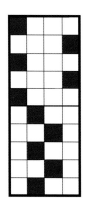

Huck Lace with Warp Floats

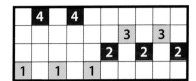

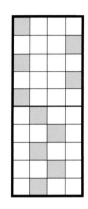

Swatches in this section shown woven with:

Warp: 5/2 cotton

Weft: 5/2 cotton

■ Wine

▨ Tea

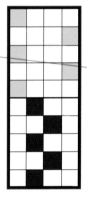

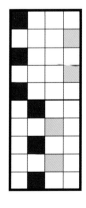

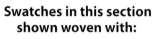

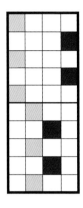

Swatches in this section
shown woven with:

Warp: 5/2 cotton

Weft: 5/2 cotton

- Wine
- Tea

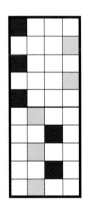

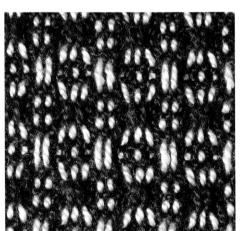

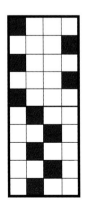

Huck Lace with Weft Floats

MONOCHROMATIC

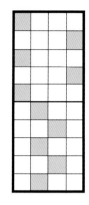

Swatches in this section shown woven with:

Warp: 5/2 cotton

Weft: 5/2 cotton

⬛ Wine

▨ Tea

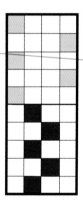

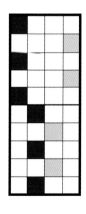

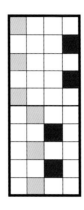

Swatches in this section
shown woven with:

Warp: 5/2 cotton

Weft: 5/2 cotton

■ Wine

▨ Tea

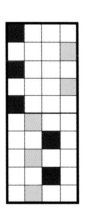

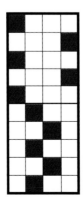

Huck Lace with Warp and Weft Floats

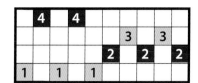

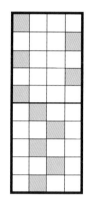

Swatches in this section shown woven with:

Warp: 5/2 cotton

Weft: 5/2 cotton

■ Wine

▨ Tea

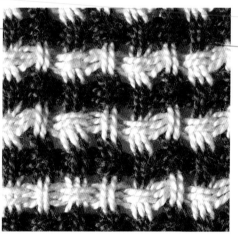

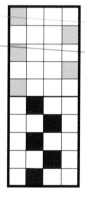

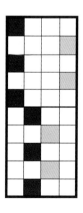

Huck Lace with Warp and Weft Floats

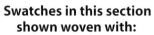

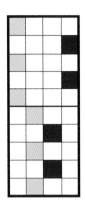

Swatches in this section
shown woven with:

Warp: 5/2 cotton

Weft: 5/2 cotton

■ Wine

▨ Tea

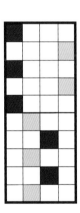

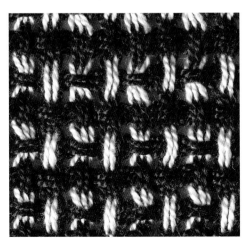

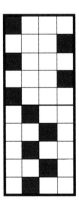

Lacy Huck Squares

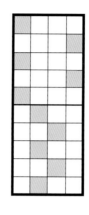

Swatches in this section shown woven with:

Warp: 5/2 cotton

Weft: 5/2 cotton

■ Wine

▨ Tea

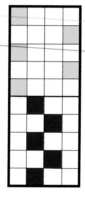

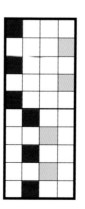

Lacy Huck Squares

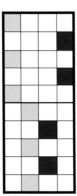

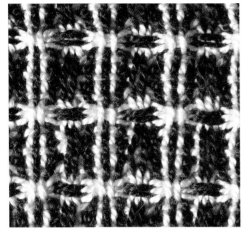

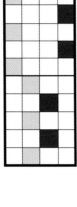

Swatches in this section shown woven with:

Warp: 5/2 cotton

Weft: 5/2 cotton

- Wine
- Tea

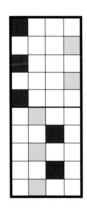

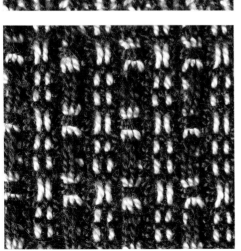

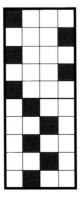

MONOCHROMATIC

Huck Lace with Warp Floats

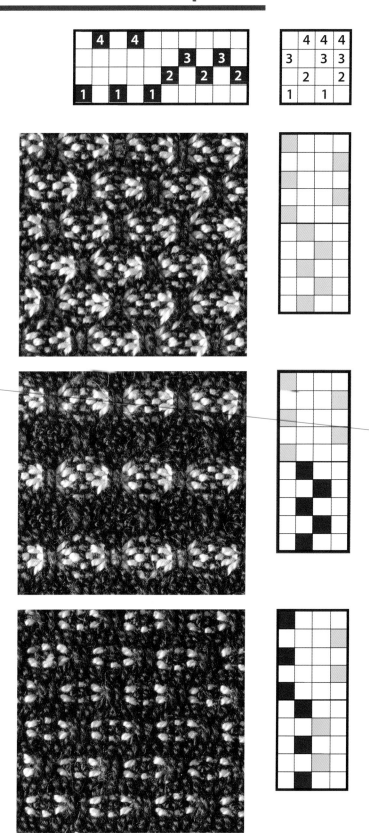

Swatches in this section shown woven with:

Warp: 5/2 cotton

Weft: 5/2 cotton

 Wine

Tea

Huck Lace with Warp Floats

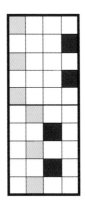

Swatches in this section shown woven with:

Warp: 5/2 cotton

Weft: 5/2 cotton

 Wine

Tea

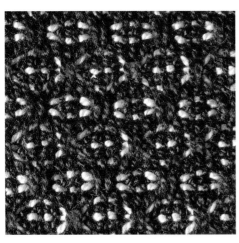
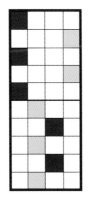

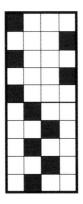

Huck Lace with Weft Floats

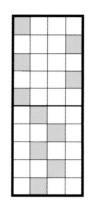

Swatches in this section shown woven with:

Warp: 5/2 cotton

Weft: 5/2 cotton

- Wine
- Tea

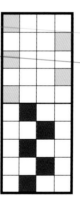

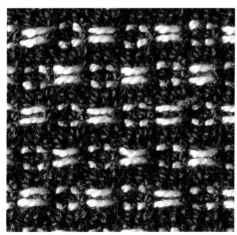

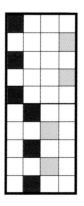

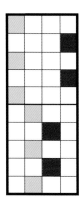

Swatches in this section shown woven with:
Warp: 5/2 cotton
Weft: 5/2 cotton

■ Wine
▨ Tea

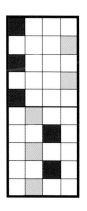

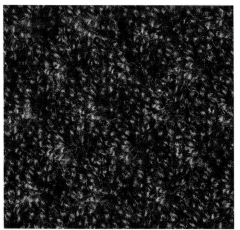
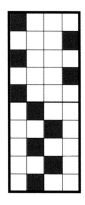

Huck Lace with Warp and Weft Floats

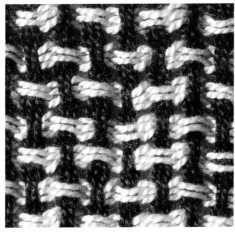

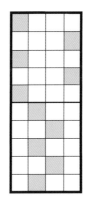

Swatches in this section shown woven with:

Warp: 5/2 cotton

Weft: 5/2 cotton

■ Wine

▨ Tea

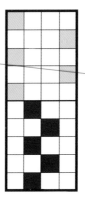

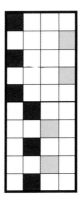

MONOCHROMATIC

Huck Lace with Warp and Weft Floats

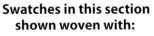

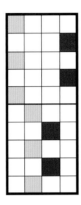

Swatches in this section shown woven with:

Warp: 5/2 cotton

Weft: 5/2 cotton

■ Wine

▨ Tea

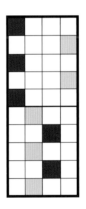

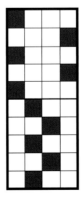

Lacy Huck Squares

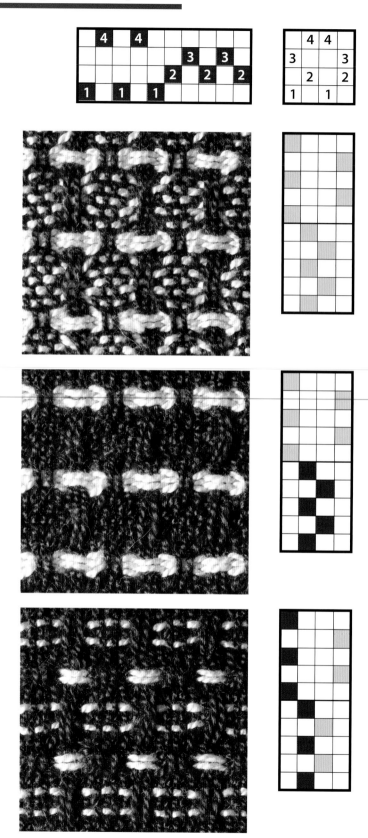

Swatches in this section shown woven with:

Warp: 5/2 cotton

Weft: 5/2 cotton

■ Wine

▨ Tea

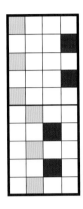

Swatches in this section shown woven with:

Warp: 5/2 cotton

Weft: 5/2 cotton

- ■ Wine
- ▨ Tea

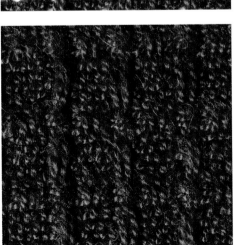

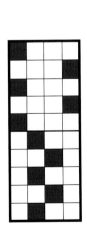

Huck Lace with Warp Floats

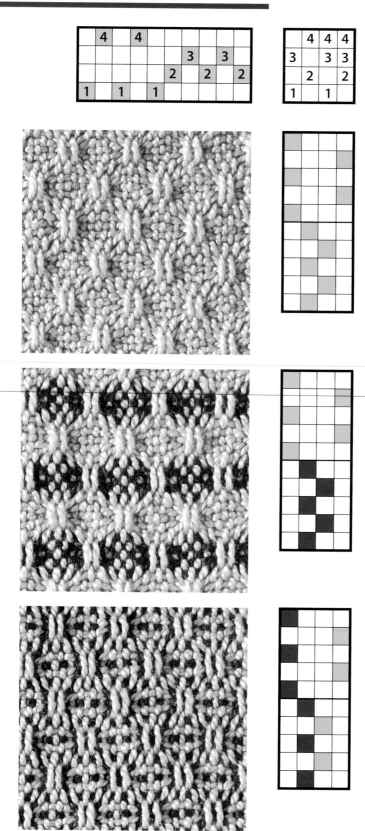

Swatches in this section shown woven with:

Warp: 5/2 cotton

Weft: 5/2 cotton

- ■ Garnet
- ▨ Kelly

Huck Lace with Warp Floats

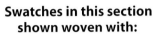

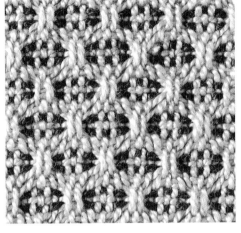

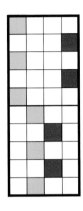

Swatches in this section shown woven with:

Warp: 5/2 cotton

Weft: 5/2 cotton

■ Garnet

■ Kelly

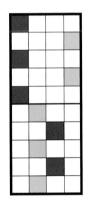

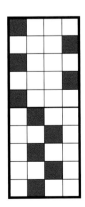

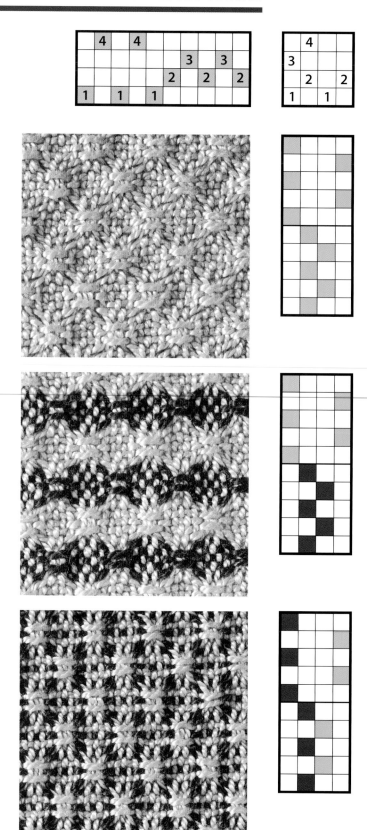

Swatches in this section
shown woven with:

Warp: 5/2 cotton

Weft: 5/2 cotton

Garnet

Kelly

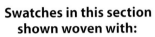

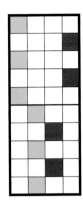

Swatches in this section shown woven with:

Warp: 5/2 cotton

Weft: 5/2 cotton

■ Garnet

□ Kelly

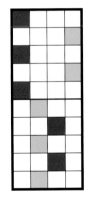

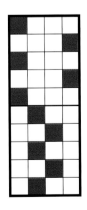

Huck Lace with Warp and Weft Floats

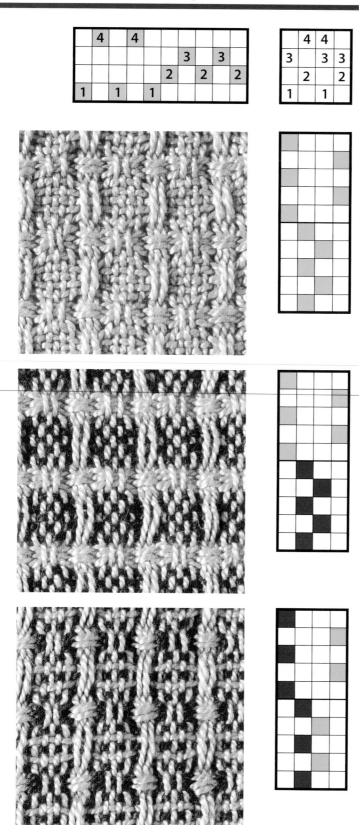

Swatches in this section shown woven with:

Warp: 5/2 cotton

Weft: 5/2 cotton

◼ Garnet

◻ Kelly

Huck Lace with Warp and Weft Floats

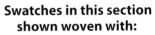

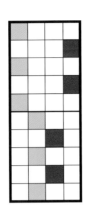

Swatches in this section shown woven with:

Warp: 5/2 cotton

Weft: 5/2 cotton

▮ Garnet

▯ Kelly

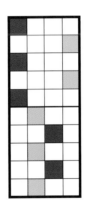

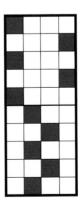

Lacy Huck Squares

COMPLEMENTARY COLORS

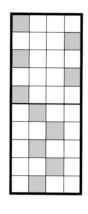

Swatches in this section shown woven with:

Warp: 5/2 cotton

Weft: 5/2 cotton

 Garnet

Kelly

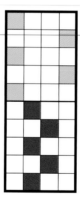

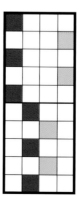

Lacy Huck Squares

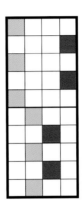

Swatches in this section shown woven with:

Warp: 5/2 cotton

Weft: 5/2 cotton

■ Garnet

□ Kelly

Huck Lace with Warp Floats

COMPLEMENTARY COLORS

Swatches in this section
shown woven with:

Warp: 5/2 cotton

Weft: 5/2 cotton

Garnet

Kelly

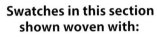

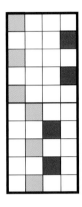

Swatches in this section shown woven with:

Warp: 5/2 cotton

Weft: 5/2 cotton

Garnet

Kelly

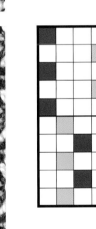

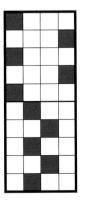

Huck Lace with Weft Floats

COMPLEMENTARY COLORS

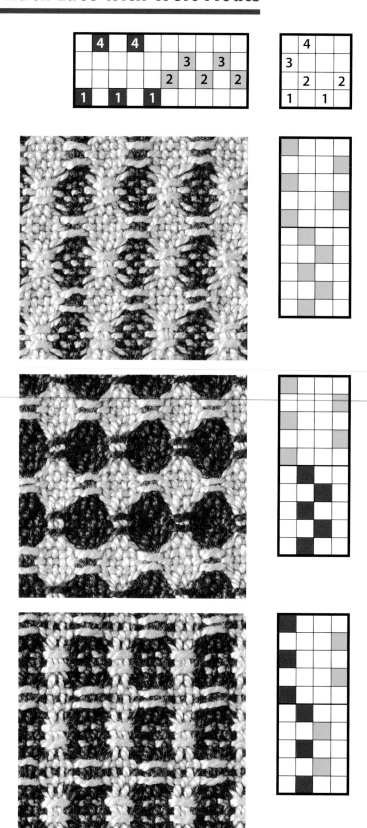

Swatches in this section shown woven with:

Warp: 5/2 cotton

Weft: 5/2 cotton

- Garnet
- Kelly

Huck Lace with Weft Floats

 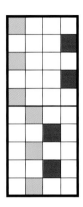

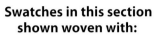

Swatches in this section shown woven with:

Warp: 5/2 cotton

Weft: 5/2 cotton

 Garnet

Kelly

 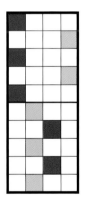

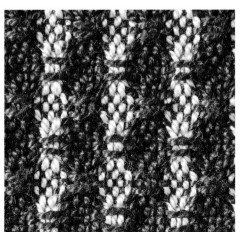 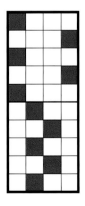

Huck Lace with Warp and Weft Floats

	4		4				
					3		3
				2		2		2
1		1		1			

	4	4
3		3	3
	2		2
1		1

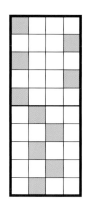

Swatches in this section shown woven with:

Warp: 5/2 cotton

Weft: 5/2 cotton

■ Garnet

▨ Kelly

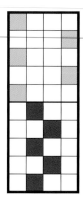

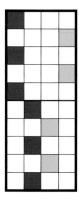

Huck Lace with Warp and Weft Floats

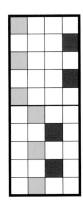

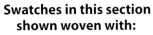

Swatches in this section shown woven with:

Warp: 5/2 cotton

Weft: 5/2 cotton

■ Garnet

▨ Kelly

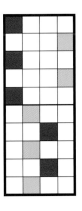

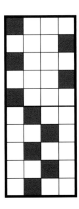

Lacy Huck Squares

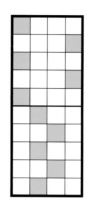

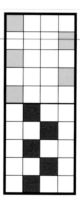

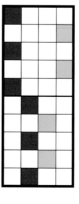

Swatches in this section shown woven with:

Warp: 5/2 cotton

Weft: 5/2 cotton

■ Garnet

▨ Kelly

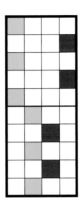

Swatches in this section shown woven with:

Warp: 5/2 cotton

Weft: 5/2 cotton

■ Garnet

▨ Kelly

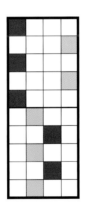

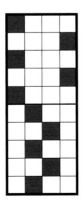

Huck Lace with Warp Floats

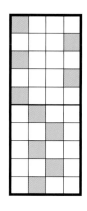

Swatches in this section shown woven with:

Warp: 5/2 cotton

Weft: 5/2 cotton

■ Garnet

■ Kelly

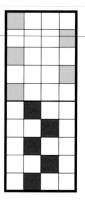

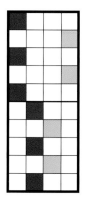

COMPLEMENTARY COLORS

Huck Lace with Warp Floats

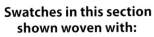

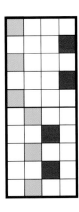

Swatches in this section shown woven with:

Warp: 5/2 cotton

Weft: 5/2 cotton

■ Garnet

▨ Kelly

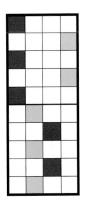

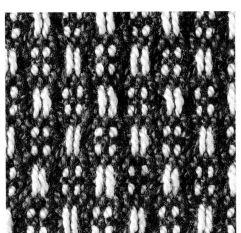
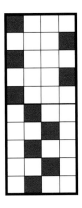

Huck Lace with Weft Floats

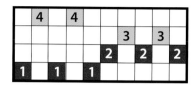

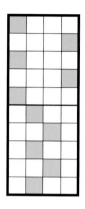

Swatches in this section shown woven with:

Warp: 5/2 cotton

Weft: 5/2 cotton

■ Garnet

▨ Kelly

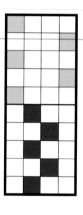

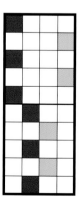

Huck Lace with Weft Floats

 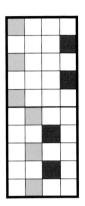

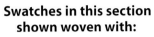

Swatches in this section shown woven with:

Warp: 5/2 cotton

Weft: 5/2 cotton

■ Garnet

▨ Kelly

 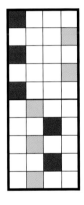

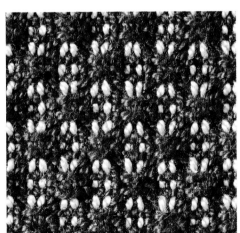 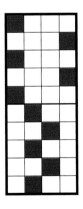

COMPLEMENTARY COLORS

Huck Lace with Warp and Weft Floats

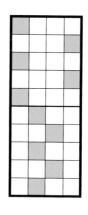

> **Swatches in this section shown woven with:**
>
> **Warp:** 5/2 cotton
>
> **Weft:** 5/2 cotton
>
> ■ Garnet
>
> ▢ Kelly

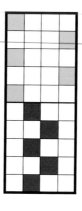

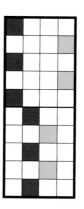

Huck Lace with Warp and Weft Floats

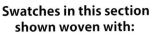

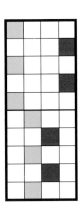

Swatches in this section shown woven with:

Warp: 5/2 cotton

Weft: 5/2 cotton

- Garnet
- Kelly

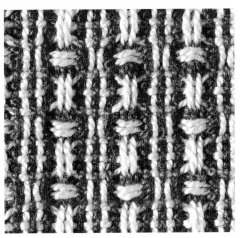

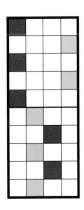

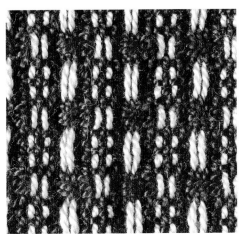

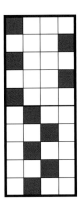

Lacy Huck Squares

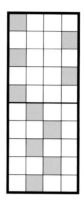

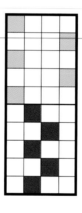

Swatches in this section shown woven with:

Warp: 5/2 cotton

Weft: 5/2 cotton

■ Garnet

■ Kelly

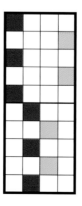

Lacy Huck Squares

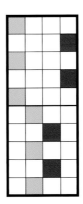

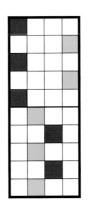

Swatches in this section
shown woven with:

Warp: 5/2 cotton

Weft: 5/2 cotton

- Garnet
- Kelly

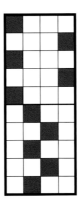

COMPLEMENTARY COLORS

Huck Lace with Warp Floats

Swatches in this section shown woven with:

Warp: 5/2 cotton

Weft: 5/2 cotton

 Garnet

Kelly

Huck Lace with Warp Floats

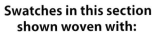

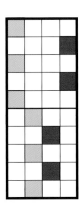

Swatches in this section shown woven with:

Warp: 5/2 cotton

Weft: 5/2 cotton

■ Garnet

▢ Kelly

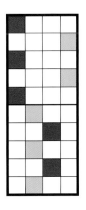

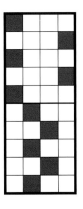

Huck Lace with Weft Floats

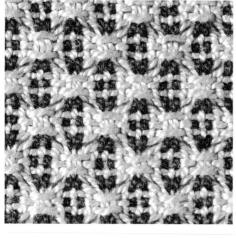

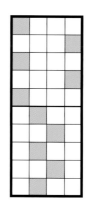

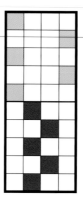

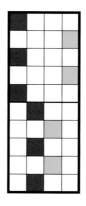

Swatches in this section shown woven with:

Warp: 5/2 cotton

Weft: 5/2 cotton

Garnet

Kelly

COMPLEMENTARY COLORS

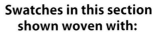

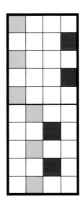

**Swatches in this section
shown woven with:**

Warp: 5/2 cotton

Weft: 5/2 cotton

■ Garnet

□ Kelly

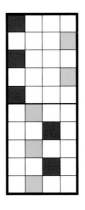

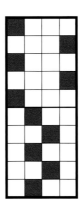

Huck Lace with Warp and Weft Floats

	4		4						
					3		3		
				2		2		2	
1		1		1					

	4	4	
3		3	3
	2		2
1		1	

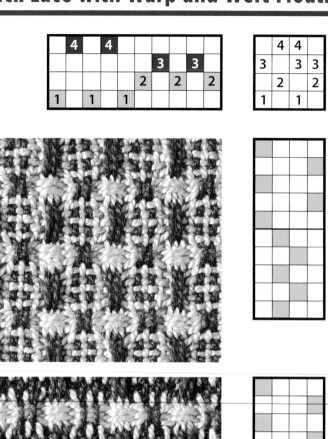

Swatches in this section shown woven with:

Warp: 5/2 cotton

Weft: 5/2 cotton

■ Garnet

▨ Kelly

Huck Lace with Warp and Weft Floats

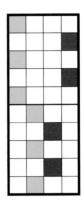

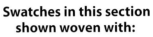

Swatches in this section shown woven with:

Warp: 5/2 cotton

Weft: 5/2 cotton

■ Garnet

□ Kelly

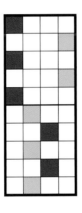

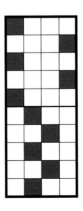

Lacy Huck Squares

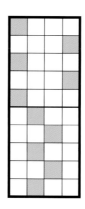

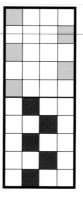

Swatches in this section shown woven with:

Warp: 5/2 cotton

Weft: 5/2 cotton

Garnet

Kelly

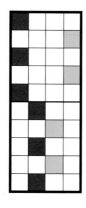

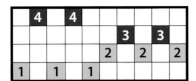

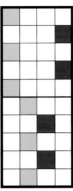

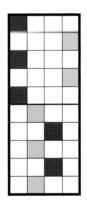

Swatches in this section shown woven with:

Warp: 5/2 cotton

Weft: 5/2 cotton

- Garnet
- Kelly

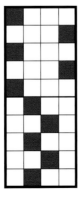

Huck Lace with Warp Floats

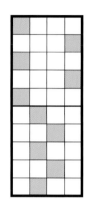

Swatches in this section shown woven with:

Warp: 5/2 cotton

Weft: 5/2 cotton

- Garnet
- Kelly

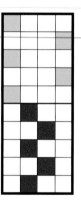

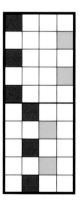

Huck Lace with Warp Floats

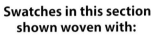

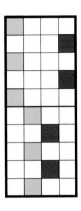

Swatches in this section shown woven with:

Warp: 5/2 cotton

Weft: 5/2 cotton

⬛ Garnet

🔲 Kelly

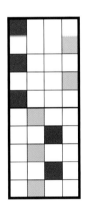

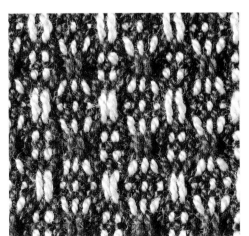

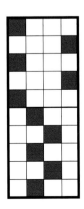

COMPLEMENTARY COLORS

HUCK LACE PATTERNS | **145**

Huck Lace with Weft Floats

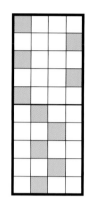

Swatches in this section shown woven with:

Warp: 5/2 cotton

Weft: 5/2 cotton

■ Garnet

▨ Kelly

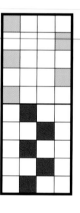

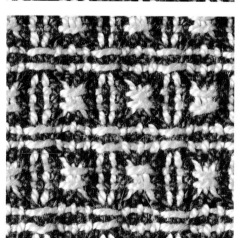

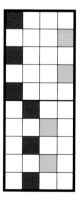

COMPLEMENTARY COLORS

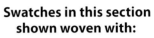

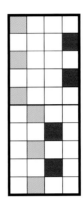

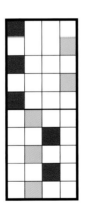

Swatches in this section shown woven with:

Warp: 5/2 cotton

Weft: 5/2 cotton

■ Garnet

▨ Kelly

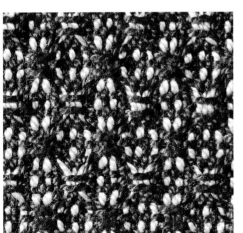

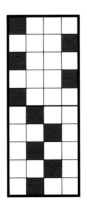

Huck Lace with Warp and Weft Floats

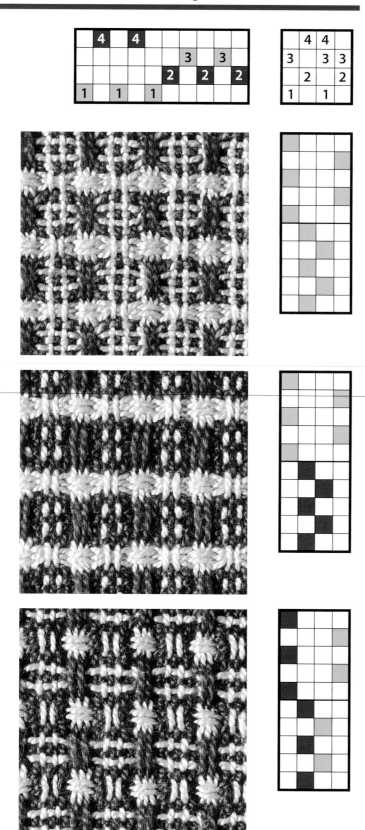

Swatches in this section shown woven with:

Warp: 5/2 cotton

Weft: 5/2 cotton

 Garnet

Kelly

Huck Lace with Warp and Weft Floats

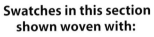

	4	4				
				3		3
			2		2		2
1		1		1			

	4	4
3		3	3
	2		2
1		1

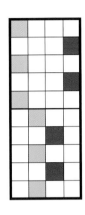

Swatches in this section shown woven with:

Warp: 5/2 cotton

Weft: 5/2 cotton

■ Garnet

■ Kelly

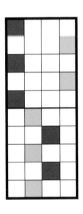

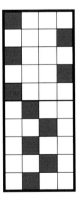

Lacy Huck Squares

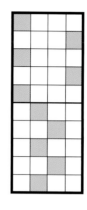

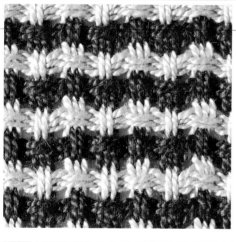

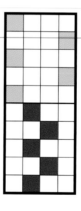

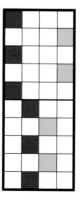

Swatches in this section shown woven with:

Warp: 5/2 cotton

Weft: 5/2 cotton

■ Garnet

▨ Kelly

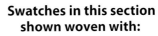

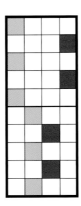

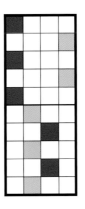

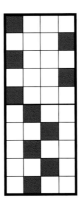

Swatches in this section shown woven with:

Warp: 5/2 cotton

Weft: 5/2 cotton

Garnet

Kelly

Huck Lace with Warp Floats

Swatches in this section shown woven with:

Warp: 5/2 cotton

Weft: 5/2 cotton

 Garnet

Kelly

Huck Lace with Warp Floats

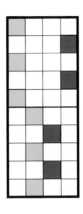

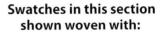

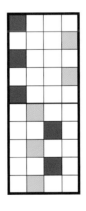

Swatches in this section shown woven with:

Warp: 5/2 cotton

Weft: 5/2 cotton

■ Garnet

■ Kelly

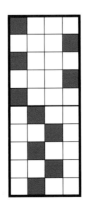

Huck Lace with Weft Floats

COMPLEMENTARY COLORS

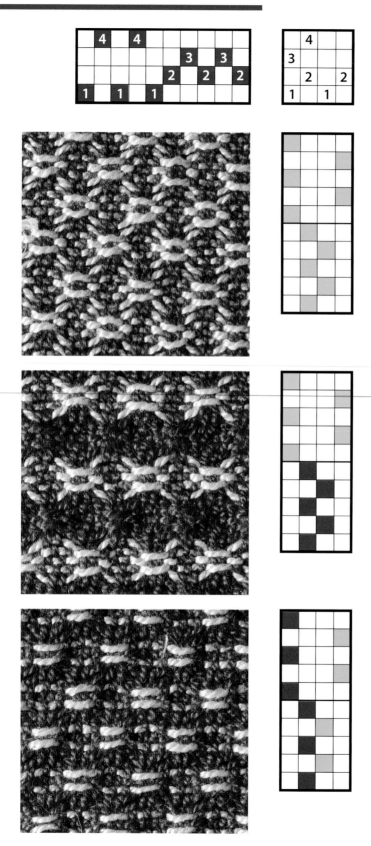

Swatches in this section shown woven with:

Warp: 5/2 cotton

Weft: 5/2 cotton

Garnet

Kelly

Huck Lace with Weft Floats

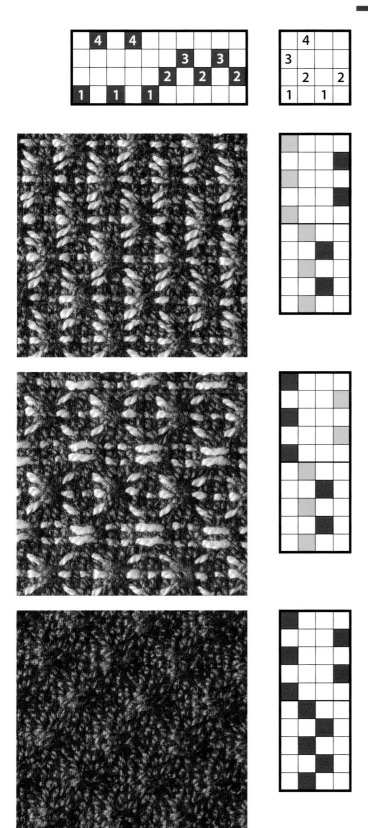

Swatches in this section shown woven with:

Warp: 5/2 cotton

Weft: 5/2 cotton

■ Garnet

▨ Kelly

Huck Lace with Warp and Weft Floats

COMPLEMENTARY COLORS

Swatches in this section shown woven with:

Warp: 5/2 cotton

Weft: 5/2 cotton

■ Garnet

□ Kelly

Huck Lace with Warp and Weft Floats

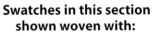

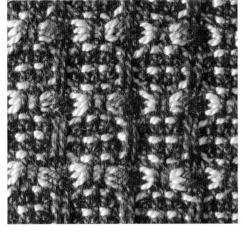
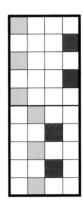

Swatches in this section shown woven with:

Warp: 5/2 cotton

Weft: 5/2 cotton

■ Garnet

▨ Kelly

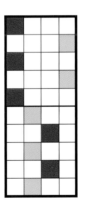

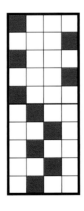

COMPLEMENTARY COLORS

Lacy Huck Squares

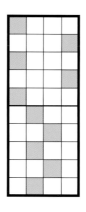

Swatches in this section shown woven with:

Warp: 5/2 cotton

Weft: 5/2 cotton

- Garnet
- Kelly

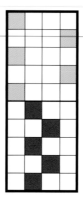

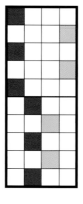

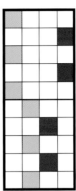

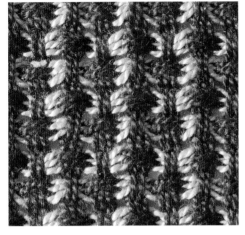

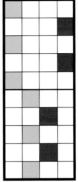

Swatches in this section shown woven with:

Warp: 5/2 cotton

Weft: 5/2 cotton

Garnet

Kelly

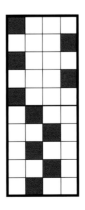

Huck Lace with Warp Floats

	4		4					
					3		3	
				2		2		2
1		1		1				

	4	4	4
3		3	3
	2		2
1		1	

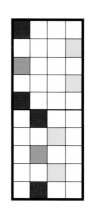

Swatches in this section shown woven with:

Warp: 5/2 cotton

Weft: 5/2 cotton

- Wine Tone
- Tangerine
- Pistachio

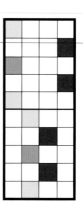

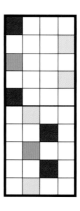

Huck Lace with Warp Floats

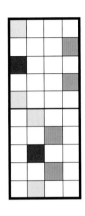

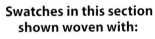

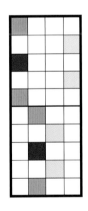

Swatches in this section shown woven with:

Warp: 5/2 cotton

Weft: 5/2 cotton

- Wine Tone
- Tangerine
- Pistachio

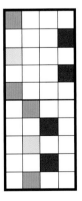

Huck Lace with Weft Floats

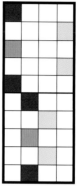

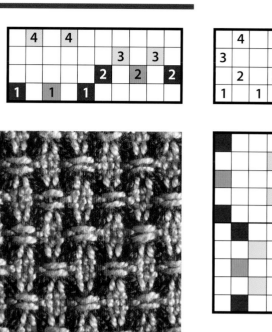

> **Swatches in this section shown woven with:**
>
> **Warp:** 5/2 cotton
>
> **Weft:** 5/2 cotton
>
> ■ Wine Tone
> ▨ Tangerine
> ▢ Pistachio

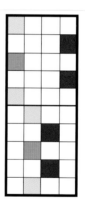

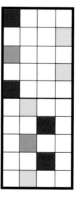

TRIADIC COLORS

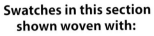

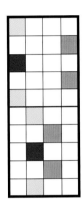

Swatches in this section shown woven with:

Warp: 5/2 cotton

Weft: 5/2 cotton

- Wine Tone
- Tangerine
- Pistachio

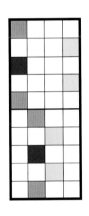

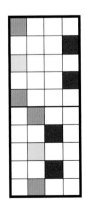

Huck Lace with Warp and Weft Floats

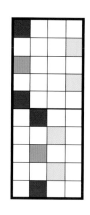

Swatches in this section shown woven with:

Warp: 5/2 cotton

Weft: 5/2 cotton

- ■ Wine Tone
- ■ Tangerine
- ■ Pistachio

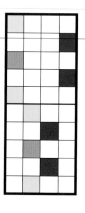

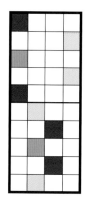

Huck Lace with Warp and Weft Floats

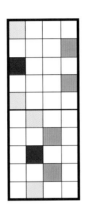

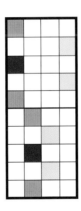

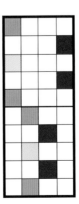

Swatches in this section shown woven with:

Warp: 5/2 cotton

Weft: 5/2 cotton

- Wine Tone
- Tangerine
- Pistachio

Lacy Huck Squares

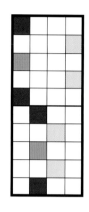

Swatches in this section shown woven with:

Warp: 5/2 cotton

Weft: 5/2 cotton

■ Wine Tone

■ Tangerine

□ Pistachio

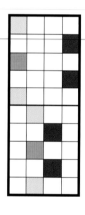

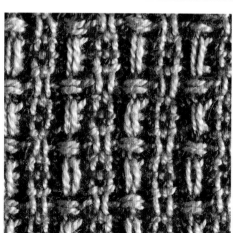

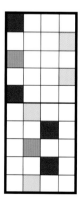

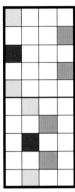

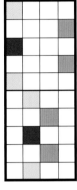

Swatches in this section shown woven with:

Warp: 5/2 cotton

Weft: 5/2 cotton

- Wine Tone
- Tangerine
- Pistachio

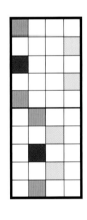

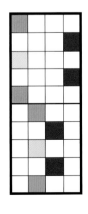

Huck Lace with Warp Floats

Swatches in this section shown woven with:

Warp: 5/2 cotton

Weft: 5/2 cotton

 Wine Tone

 Tangerine

Pistachio

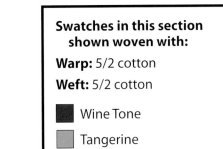

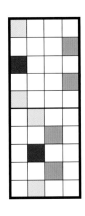

Swatches in this section shown woven with:

Warp: 5/2 cotton

Weft: 5/2 cotton

- ■ Wine Tone
- ■ Tangerine
- ■ Pistachio

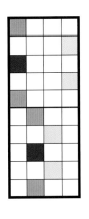

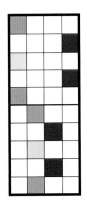

Huck Lace with Weft Floats

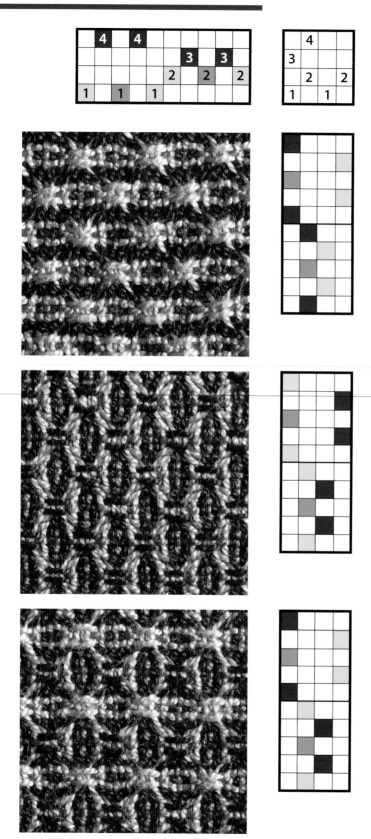

Swatches in this section
shown woven with:

Warp: 5/2 cotton

Weft: 5/2 cotton

- Wine Tone
- Tangerine
- Pistachio

Huck Lace with Weft Floats

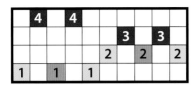

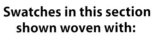

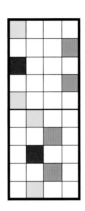

Swatches in this section shown woven with:

Warp: 5/2 cotton

Weft: 5/2 cotton

Wine Tone

Tangerine

Pistachio

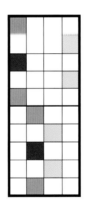

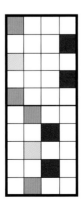

Huck Lace with Warp and Weft Floats

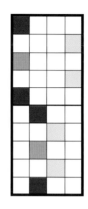

Swatches in this section shown woven with:

Warp: 5/2 cotton

Weft: 5/2 cotton

■ Wine Tone

■ Tangerine

□ Pistachio

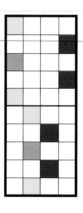

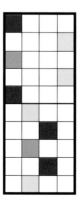

Huck Lace with Warp and Weft Floats

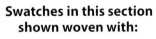

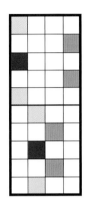

Swatches in this section shown woven with:

Warp: 5/2 cotton

Weft: 5/2 cotton

- ■ Wine Tone
- ▤ Tangerine
- ▥ Pistachio

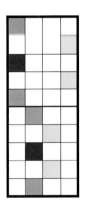

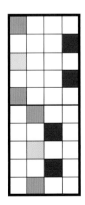

Lacy Huck Squares

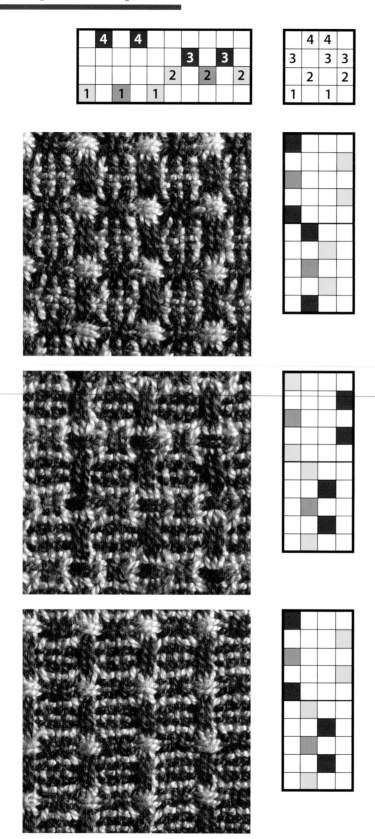

Swatches in this section shown woven with:

Warp: 5/2 cotton

Weft: 5/2 cotton

- Wine Tone
- Tangerine
- Pistachio

Lacy Huck Squares

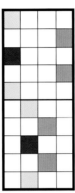

Swatches in this section shown woven with:

Warp: 5/2 cotton

Weft: 5/2 cotton

- ■ Wine Tone
- ■ Tangerine
- □ Pistachio

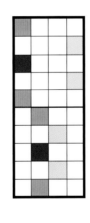

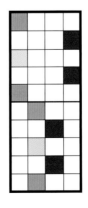

Huck Lace with Warp Floats

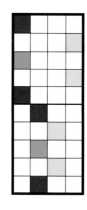

Swatches in this section shown woven with:

Warp: 5/2 cotton

Weft: 5/2 cotton

■ Wine Tone

■ Tangerine

□ Pistachio

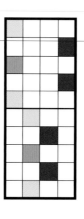

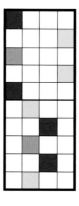

Huck Lace with Warp Floats

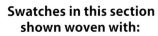

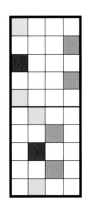

Swatches in this section shown woven with:

Warp: 5/2 cotton

Weft: 5/2 cotton

■ Wine Tone

■ Tangerine

□ Pistachio

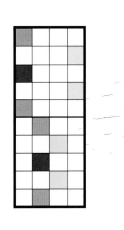

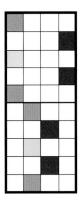

Huck Lace with Weft Floats

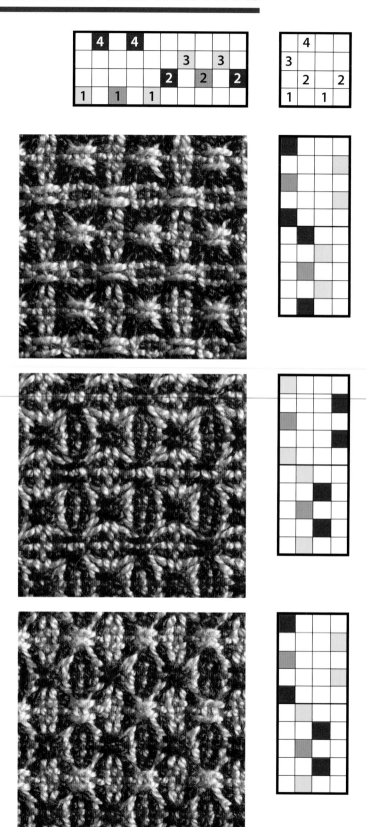

Swatches in this section shown woven with:

Warp: 5/2 cotton

Weft: 5/2 cotton

- ■ Wine Tone
- ■ Tangerine
- □ Pistachio

Huck Lace with Weft Floats

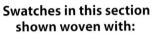

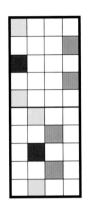

Swatches in this section shown woven with:

Warp: 5/2 cotton

Weft: 5/2 cotton

- Wine Tone
- Tangerine
- Pistachio

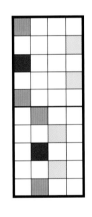

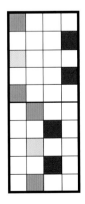

Huck Lace with Warp and Weft Floats

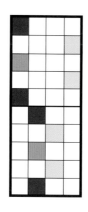

Swatches in this section shown woven with:

Warp: 5/2 cotton

Weft: 5/2 cotton

- Wine Tone
- Tangerine
- Pistachio

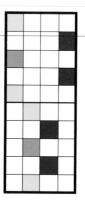

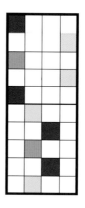

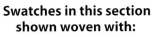

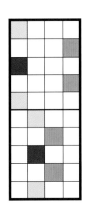

Swatches in this section shown woven with:

Warp: 5/2 cotton

Weft: 5/2 cotton

- Wine Tone
- Tangerine
- Pistachio

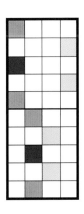

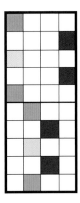

Lacy Huck Squares

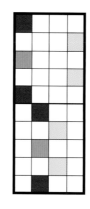

Swatches in this section shown woven with:

Warp: 5/2 cotton

Weft: 5/2 cotton

■ Wine Tone

■ Tangerine

□ Pistachio

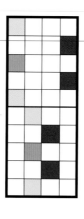

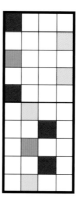

		4	4		
	3			3	3
			2		2
	1			1	

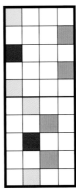

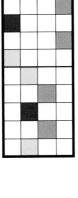

Swatches in this section shown woven with:

Warp: 5/2 cotton

Weft: 5/2 cotton

- Wine Tone
- Tangerine
- Pistachio

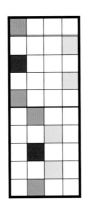

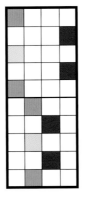

Huck Lace with Warp Floats

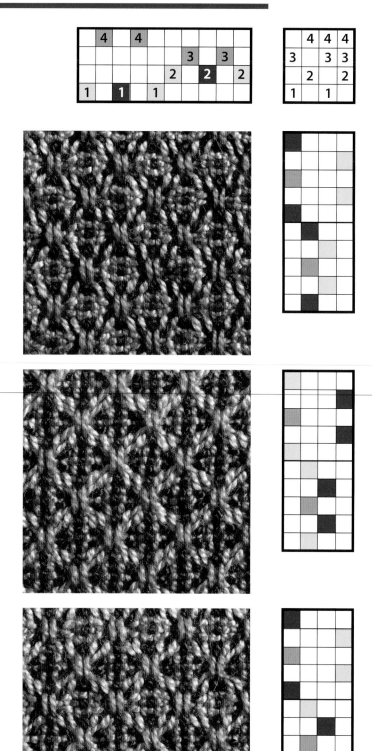

Swatches in this section shown woven with:

Warp: 5/2 cotton

Weft: 5/2 cotton

- Wine Tone
- Tangerine
- Pistachio

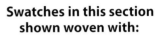

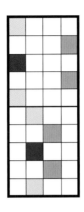

Swatches in this section shown woven with:

Warp: 5/2 cotton

Weft: 5/2 cotton

- Wine Tone
- Tangerine
- Pistachio

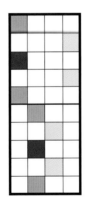

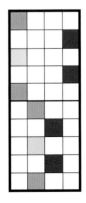

Huck Lace with Weft Floats

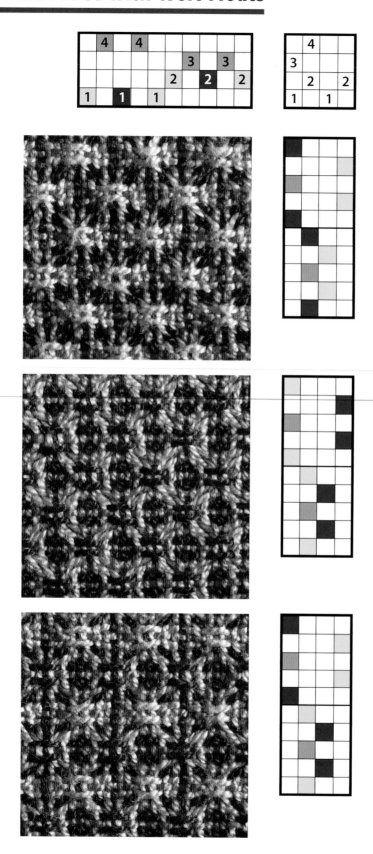

Swatches in this section shown woven with:

Warp: 5/2 cotton

Weft: 5/2 cotton

- Wine Tone
- Tangerine
- Pistachio

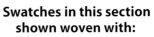

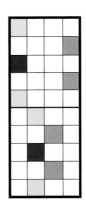

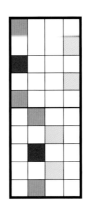

Swatches in this section shown woven with:

Warp: 5/2 cotton

Weft: 5/2 cotton

- Wine Tone
- Tangerine
- Pistachio

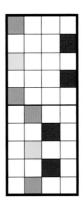

Huck Lace with Warp and Weft Floats

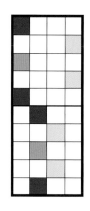

Swatches in this section shown woven with:

Warp: 5/2 cotton

Weft: 5/2 cotton

- Wine Tone
- Tangerine
- Pistachio

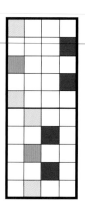

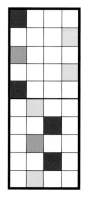

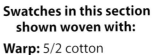

Huck Lace with Warp and Weft Floats

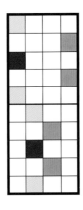

Swatches in this section shown woven with:

Warp: 5/2 cotton

Weft: 5/2 cotton

- Wine Tone
- Tangerine
- Pistachio

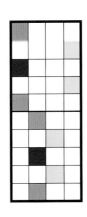

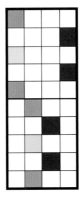

Lacy Huck Squares

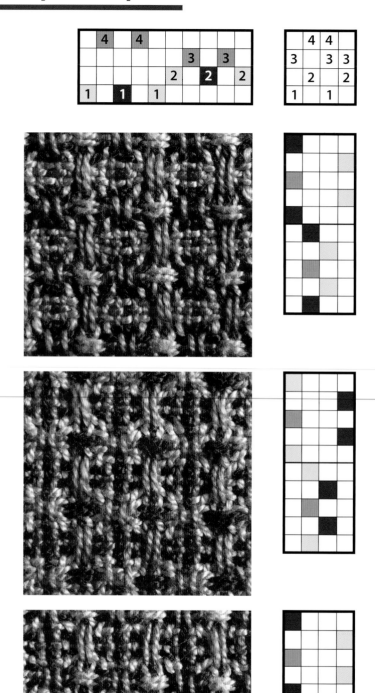

Swatches in this section shown woven with:

Warp: 5/2 cotton

Weft: 5/2 cotton

- Wine Tone
- Tangerine
- Pistachio

Lacy Huck Squares

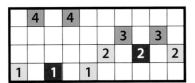

	4	4	
3		3	3
	2		2
1		1	

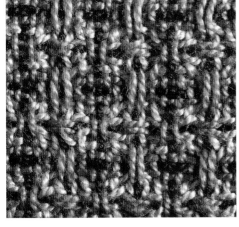
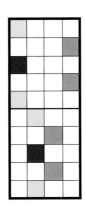

Swatches in this section shown woven with:

Warp: 5/2 cotton

Weft: 5/2 cotton

- ■ Wine Tone
- ▨ Tangerine
- ▫ Pistachio

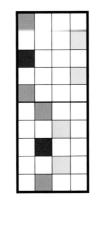

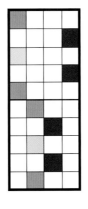

Huck Lace with Warp Floats

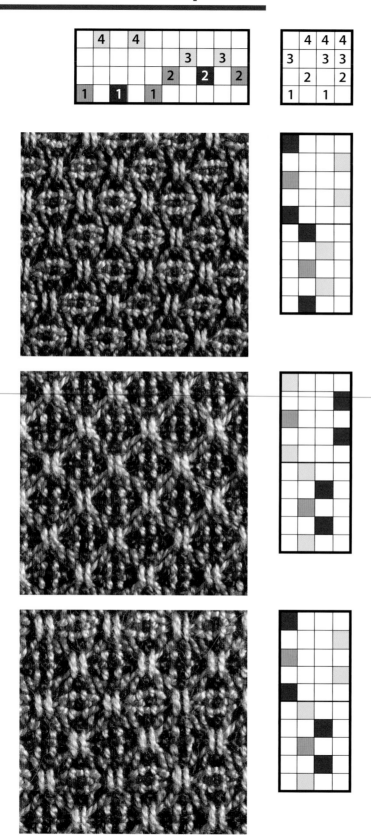

Swatches in this section shown woven with:

Warp: 5/2 cotton

Weft: 5/2 cotton

- Wine Tone
- Tangerine
- Pistachio

Huck Lace with Warp Floats

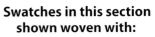

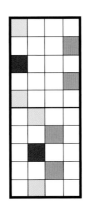

Swatches in this section shown woven with:

Warp: 5/2 cotton

Weft: 5/2 cotton

- Wine Tone
- Tangerine
- Pistachio

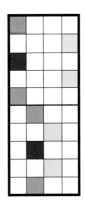

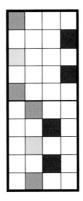

Huck Lace with Weft Floats

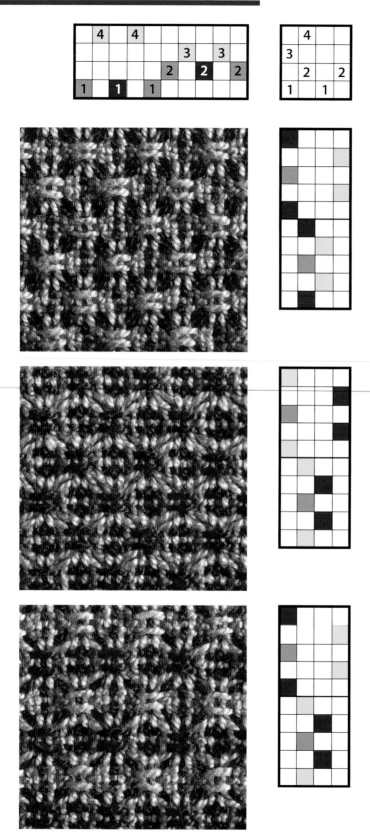

Swatches in this section shown woven with:

Warp: 5/2 cotton

Weft: 5/2 cotton

- ■ Wine Tone
- ▨ Tangerine
- ▢ Pistachio

Huck Lace with Weft Floats

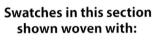

	4		4						
						3		3	
					2		2		2
1		1		1					

	4		
3			
		2	2
1		1	

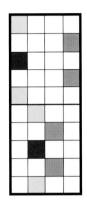

Swatches in this section shown woven with:

Warp: 5/2 cotton

Weft: 5/2 cotton

- ⬛ Wine Tone
- ⬛ Tangerine
- ⬜ Pistachio

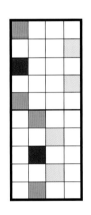

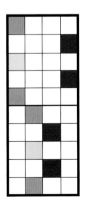

TRIADIC COLORS

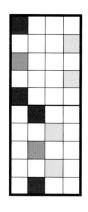

Swatches in this section shown woven with:

Warp: 5/2 cotton

Weft: 5/2 cotton

- Wine Tone
- Tangerine
- Pistachio

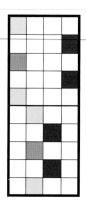

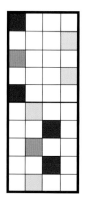

Huck Lace with Warp and Weft Floats

	4		4					
						3		3
					2		2		2
1		1		1				

		4	4	
3				3
		2		2
1		1		

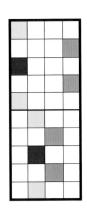

Swatches in this section shown woven with:

Warp: 5/2 cotton

Weft: 5/2 cotton

- Wine Tone
- Tangerine
- Pistachio

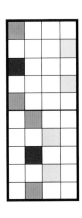

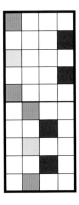

Lacy Huck Squares

TRIADIC COLORS

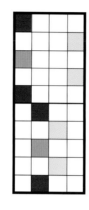

Swatches in this section shown woven with:

Warp: 5/2 cotton

Weft: 5/2 cotton

- Wine Tone
- Tangerine
- Pistachio

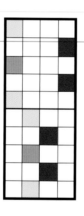

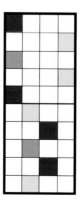

Lacy Huck Squares

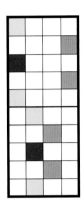

Swatches in this section shown woven with:

Warp: 5/2 cotton

Weft: 5/2 cotton

- Wine Tone
- Tangerine
- Pistachio

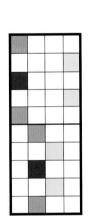

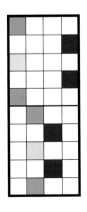

Huck Lace with Warp Floats

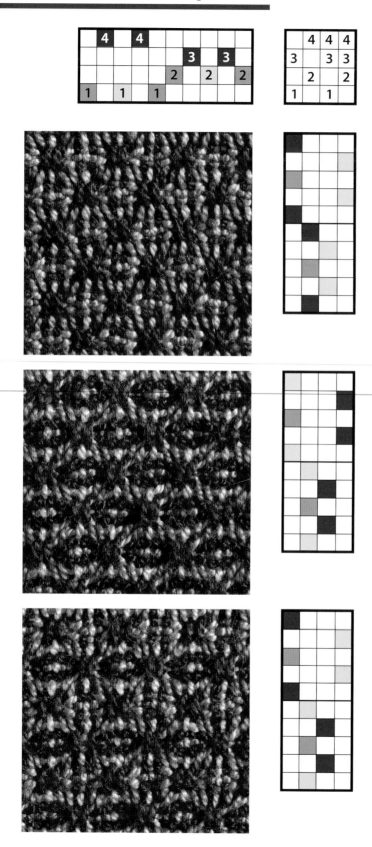

Swatches in this section shown woven with:

Warp: 5/2 cotton

Weft: 5/2 cotton

 Wine Tone

Tangerine

Pistachio

Huck Lace with Warp Floats

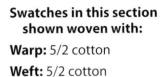

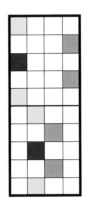

Swatches in this section shown woven with:

Warp: 5/2 cotton

Weft: 5/2 cotton

- Wine Tone
- Tangerine
- Pistachio

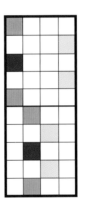

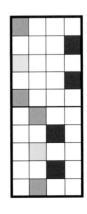

Huck Lace with Weft Floats

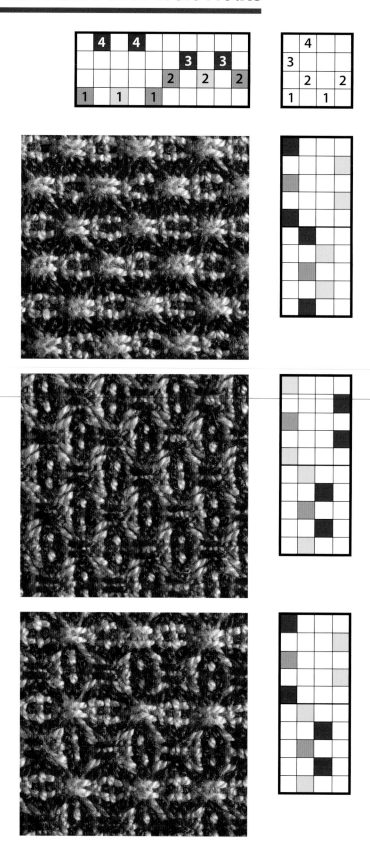

Swatches in this section shown woven with:

Warp: 5/2 cotton

Weft: 5/2 cotton

- Wine Tone
- Tangerine
- Pistachio

Huck Lace with Weft Floats

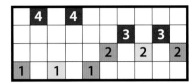

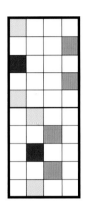

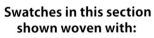

Swatches in this section shown woven with:

Warp: 5/2 cotton

Weft: 5/2 cotton

- Wine Tone
- Tangerine
- Pistachio

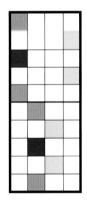

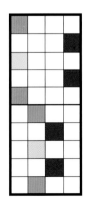

Huck Lace with Warp and Weft Floats

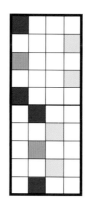

Swatches in this section shown woven with:

Warp: 5/2 cotton

Weft: 5/2 cotton

■ Wine Tone

■ Tangerine

□ Pistachio

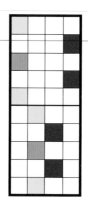

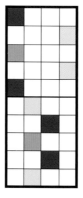

Huck Lace with Warp and Weft Floats

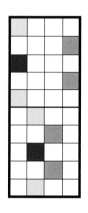

Swatches in this section shown woven with:

Warp: 5/2 cotton

Weft: 5/2 cotton

- ■ Wine Tone
- ■ Tangerine
- ▢ Pistachio

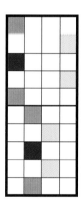

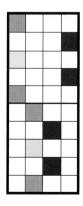

Lacy Huck Squares

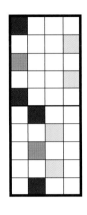

Swatches in this section shown woven with:

Warp: 5/2 cotton

Weft: 5/2 cotton

- Wine Tone
- Tangerine
- Pistachio

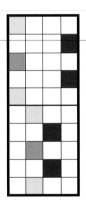

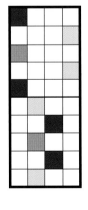

Lacy Huck Squares

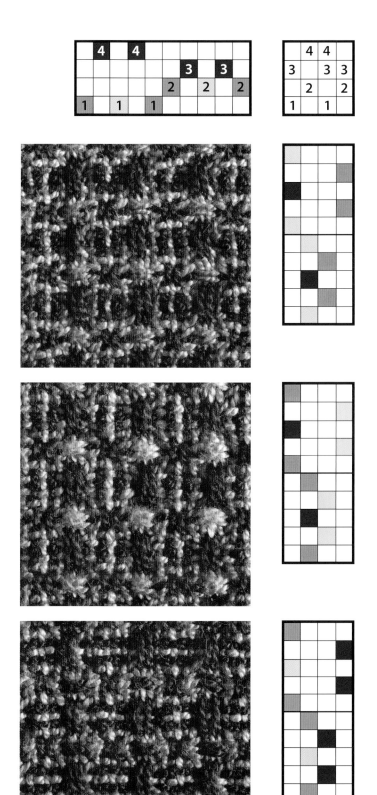

Swatches in this section shown woven with:

Warp: 5/2 cotton

Weft: 5/2 cotton

- ■ Wine Tone
- ■ Tangerine
- ■ Pistachio

HUCK PROJECTS

I feel that it is one thing to offer you this pattern study of color and weave effects on Huck but quite another to add a few projects to show you how to use this reference. Here are a few simple projects for you to try, using a variety of different threads. Let this only be a start in your exploration of Huck. Like recipes, tweak them to make them your own. Change the threads; make the warps wider or longer. Keep good records of what you have done, and make sure that you share your results with others. Some people like large kitchen towels, and others like small towels. The mug rugs or cocktail carpets are fun to weave and make a great gift to give with a pottery mug or martini glass.

I have been asked why I didn't include the length of the place mats in my book *Handwoven Table Linens*. I also didn't tell the reader how long to make the warp, because each person might have a different idea of how big a place mat should be. My mother had a round oak kitchen table, and she found it hard to find a place mat that fit her table. Long place mats that work on a rectangular table didn't work on hers because the corners drooped off the edge. I wove shorter mats for her table. The warp length will also depend on how many place mats you want to weave. In a case such as this, find a place mat (or whatever item you are weaving) that you like and measure it. Then add adjustments for hems and take-up, and multiply that figure by the number of items you wish to weave. Don't forget to add loom waste and, if you want to sample, add a yard or so for experimentation. There you have it. Pick a beginning project and warp up your loom, and remember to always enjoy your weaving.

PROJECT 1:
Tencel Scarf

THIS IS A MARRIAGE MADE IN HEAVEN: the combination of using Tencel for the warp and weft and then adding your newfound knowledge of Huck with color and weave effects. As with all Huck, you are going to see warp floats on one side of the scarf and weft floats on the other. The scarf will have two equally beautiful patterns, but different on each side.

I chose to use a monochromatic theme with this scarf. I used dark and light red-based threads, but you can, of course, use any color mix you like. I believe that solid colors will work best. I mention this because there are numerous variegated, space-dyed Tencel threads out there, and they are beautiful and tempting to use. The results, however, might weave up with a muddy look and finish to the fabric. If you think you might want to test this, try using a very strong contrast of colors (perhaps a dark variegated combined with Lemon Yellow or Lime Green).

The addition of fabric softener in the final wash rinse will make this scarf soft and drapey. Scarves like this would make lovely gifts for special friends.

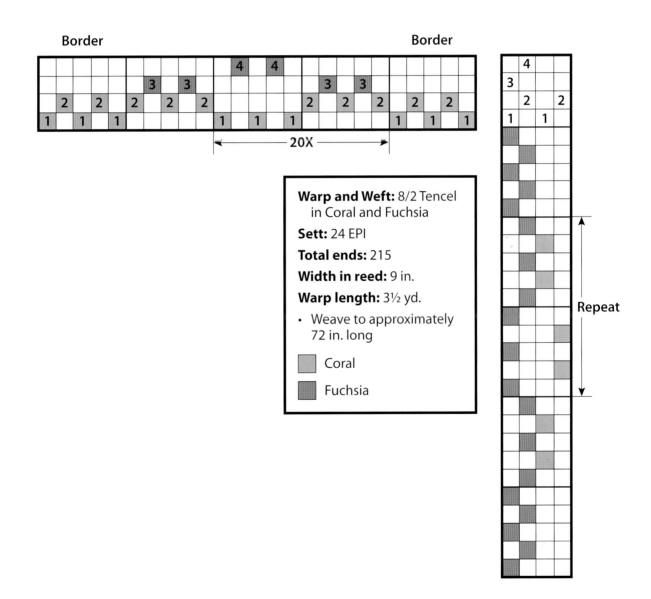

Warp and Weft: 8/2 Tencel in Coral and Fuchsia

Sett: 24 EPI

Total ends: 215

Width in reed: 9 in.

Warp length: 3½ yd.

- Weave to approximately 72 in. long

Coral

Fuchsia

PROJECT 2:
Huck Towels

TOWELS ARE FUN TO WEAVE and make the perfect gift for an appreciative cook. I personally love it when I can warp my loom and develop numerous different patterns from the same threading. In these samples, all I did was change the color order in the treadling. I used the same color threads in the weft and the warp. Try switching out one of the weft colors for something surprisingly different. Navy blue, or maybe tangerine, or even peach might be to your liking. Make the warp nice and long because you will never run out of ideas with this. I was once reminded by a friend that even a less than desirable color combination will still dry dishes. How true!

I love getting handwoven dish towels for my kitchen. There are stories and fond memories associated with each one in my drawer. I have a few towels that were given to me by weaving friends who have long since passed away. Looking at these towels keeps their memory alive. As you weave your towels, remember to bless them with a few good wishes.

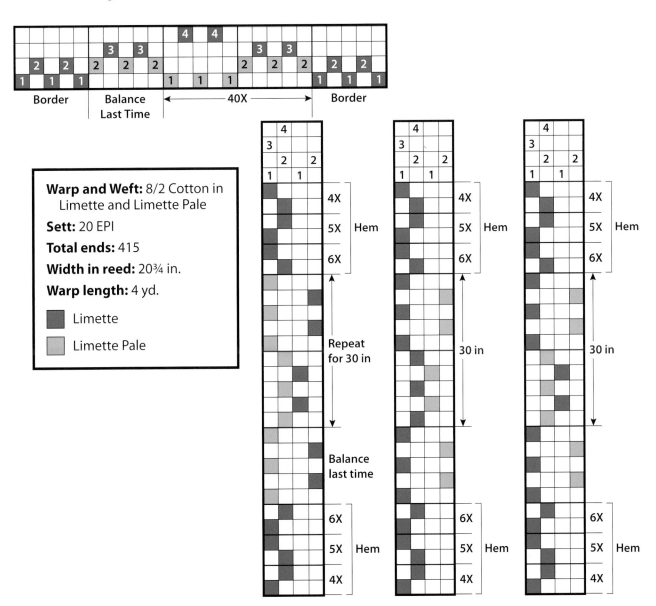

Warp and Weft: 8/2 Cotton in Limette and Limette Pale

Sett: 20 EPI

Total ends: 415

Width in reed: 20¾ in.

Warp length: 4 yd.

Limette

Limette Pale

PROJECT 3:
Baby Blanket

IF I SAY SO MYSELF, THIS IS A FABULOUS PROJECT to weave on so many levels. It nudges the beginning weaver to warp their loom at a little wider width than the normal beginner projects. But please don't fear; this is an easy project to weave and so much fun. Over all my years of teaching students to weave, I've learned that baby blankets are one of the top 10 projects on their lists. Everyone seems to know someone who is having a baby.

One day a former student came into the studio and asked for help. Five women in his office were expecting, and he wanted to weave a baby blanket for each one of those little bundles of joy. "What can I use?" he asked. "I want something that is easily washed and dried and comes in lots of colors." I have found that cotton is easy to work with, and I suggested that he use 8/4 cotton carpet warp. "But that's for rag rugs," he said. Yes, but it also works very well when woven in both the warp and the weft, and it washes to a soft, beautiful hand.

Presented here is my suggestion for a Huck blanket in gender-neutral colors. If you have a different color scheme in mind, of course you can use the same threading draft with the colors of your choice or the color preference of the expectant parents. Weave a little love into each row.

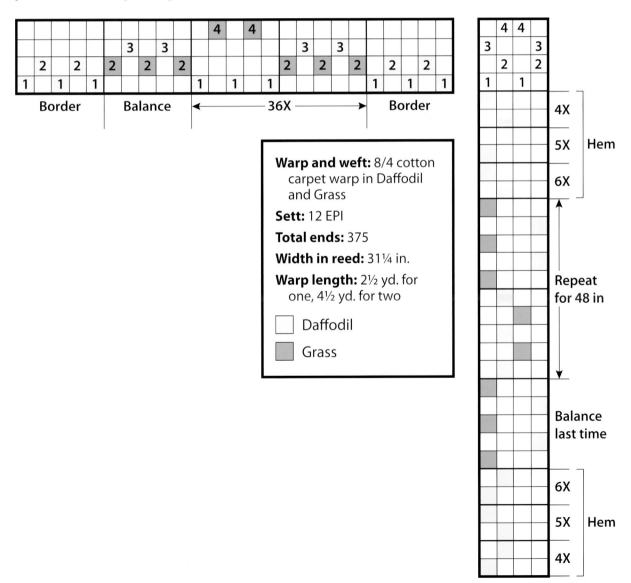

Warp and weft: 8/4 cotton carpet warp in Daffodil and Grass

Sett: 12 EPI

Total ends: 375

Width in reed: 31¼ in.

Warp length: 2½ yd. for one, 4½ yd. for two

☐ Daffodil

▨ Grass

PROJECT 4:

Huck Scarf with Texture

HERE IS A DRAFT FOR A SCARF that not only employs the idea of color and weave effects on Huck but also adds some textural interest to it. The idea is to use two different-sized threads in the warp. I used Tencel for the basic ground foundation to give the scarf drape. I then thought to put a heavier weight thread on shafts 3 and 4, the pattern shafts, to give the pattern a noticeable texture that makes people wonder how it is woven. The heavier thread is a 2/10 merino wool and Tencel blend. By sleying the entire Huck unit within one dent of the reed, it also helps to push the idea of adding texture. The weft is simply woven with the finer-weight Tencel.

The idea of adding texture to this time-honored weave structure is certainly a more modern approach to weaving Huck. You might want to try weaving textures into towels or table linens. How about a cotton baby blanket woven with two weights of thread such as 8/2 or 10/2 cotton working with a heavier 8/4 cotton? The sky is the limit!

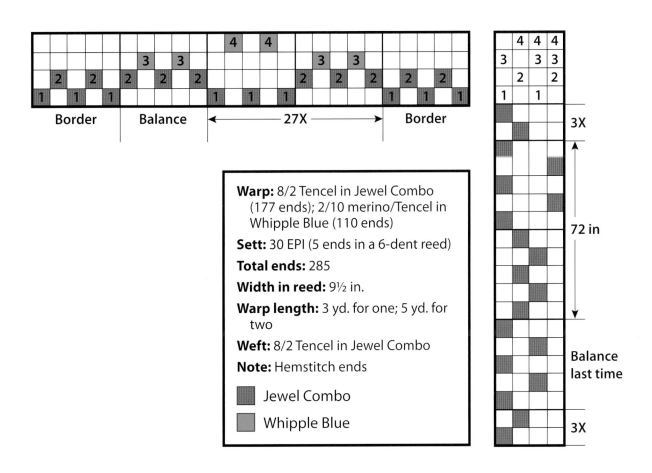

Warp: 8/2 Tencel in Jewel Combo (177 ends); 2/10 merino/Tencel in Whipple Blue (110 ends)

Sett: 30 EPI (5 ends in a 6-dent reed)

Total ends: 285

Width in reed: 9½ in.

Warp length: 3 yd. for one; 5 yd. for two

Weft: 8/2 Tencel in Jewel Combo

Note: Hemstitch ends

▉ Jewel Combo

▉ Whipple Blue

PROJECT 5:
Mug Rugs

HERE IS A QUICK LITTLE PROJECT to try weaving Huck with color and weave effects. These mug rugs are easy to warp and fast to weave. A mug rug is the perfect gift to give with a hand-thrown mug. I designed this set of mug rugs with a Southwest theme, using turquoise blue and red on a tan background. Maybe you want to pick colors to match your existing dishes. How about your school colors and a mug from the university store?

I like using 8/4 poly/cotton. The addition of polyester to the cotton warp thread makes it possible to maintain a good-looking fringe after many washings. I think a short fringe just looks appropriate on these cute little mats. If you hemstitch your mats while on the loom, it makes it easier to trim the fringe later. A self-healing mat and a rotary cutter will make cutting fringe a breeze.

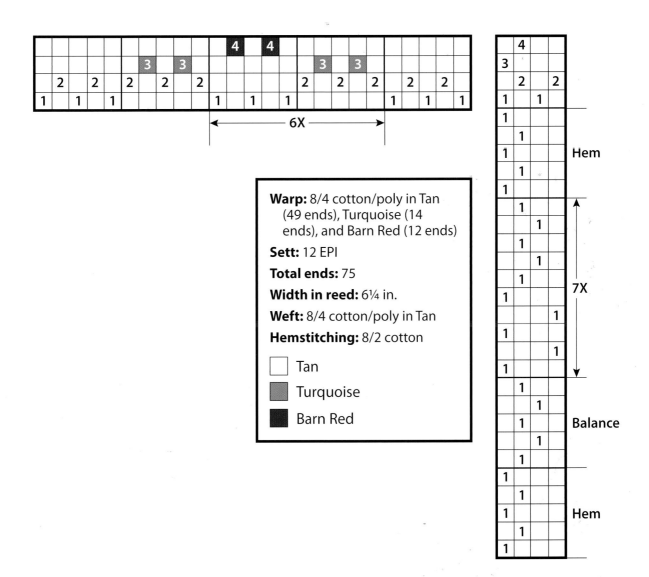

Warp: 8/4 cotton/poly in Tan (49 ends), Turquoise (14 ends), and Barn Red (12 ends)

Sett: 12 EPI

Total ends: 75

Width in reed: 6¼ in.

Weft: 8/4 cotton/poly in Tan

Hemstitching: 8/2 cotton

☐ Tan

▨ Turquoise

■ Barn Red

ACKNOWLEDGMENTS

I t's hard to close the book here because there are still so many thoughts that constantly keep coming to mind. If I keep saying, "But wait, there is something else to add," I am afraid that this work will not be published. For now, we will start with this and add a second volume if the need arises.

There are so many people in my blessed life for whom I am truly grateful. My family, my friends, and the students I teach add richness to my world. Your encouragement spurs me on to keep reaching for the next unknown thing and makes me ask myself, "What if?"

The following people were so helpful in the creating of this book. First, I want to thank my friend Madelyn van der Hoogt, who unknowingly made me look at Huck Lace with a different set of eyes. I went from the collector of antique examples to the enthusiastic weaver of my own interpretations of Huck Lace. Madelyn, thank you so much. Thanks to Candi Derr, my editor, for encouraging me to write this book. This is my fourth book, and after finishing my third on weaving linens, Candi said, "OK, what's next?"

With my busy schedule, I have to rely on the help of other weavers to weave the ideas in my head and make the samples possible. Thank you to Susan Kesler Simpson, Cindy Koedoot-Knisely, Nancy Garden, Vicky Haas, and Vonnie Davis for taking my threads and drafts and weaving them into reality. Thanks also go to the photographers, Alan Wycheck and Kathy Eckhaus, for your talents with the camera.

A special thank you goes to my daughter, Sara Bixler, who has given me countless suggestions on color when I have doubts. Sara has always been correct and sees color combinations like no one else I know. Sara also has the same drive and passion for textiles that I have, and I feel so lucky to be able to share this with her. In the calendar of life, I represent the fall and Sara is the budding spring. There is so much of her yet to come.

Lastly, I want to give thanks to the unknown Japanese weaver who wove that magnificent example of Log Cabin with the five-thread repeat. I know for a fact that this journey would never have happened had I not come across that fabric.